A GLOBAL GUIDE TO FINTECH AND FUTURE PAYMENT TRENDS

Being able to make and receive payments is an essential facet of modern life. It is integral to the banking and finance systems, and it touches all global citizens. In some areas, payment systems are rapidly evolving – moving swiftly from paper payment instruments, to electronic, to real-time – but in others, underdeveloped payment systems hold back economic and social development.

This book is intended to assist the reader in navigating the payments landscape. The author explores highly topical areas, such as the role of payment systems in enabling commerce to contribute to the development of emerging economies, the evolution of payment systems from paper instruments to computerization, the role of cryptocurrencies, and the slow decline of plastic credit and debit cards owing to alternative forms of payment being introduced.

Altogether, this book provides a comprehensive overview of the evolution of payment and offers projections for the future, encouraging readers to explore their own predictions, using the framework that the book has provided. It is vital reading for technologists, marketers, executives and investors in the FinTech sector, as well as academics teaching business and technology courses.

Peter Goldfinch is a payments specialist who has developed extensive business and technical knowledge from delivering solutions. In 1991, he co-founded the GFG Group, a consultancy and services company. In the mid-2000s, GFG became a payments and cards product company that was sold in 2014 to Wirecard. In 2002, he left GFG and joined Visa Asia Pacific as CTO Domestic Processing before rejoining the GFG in 2005 as General Manager for Asia. In 2010, Peter returned to consultancy.

Innovation and Technology Horizons

Series Editor

Vanessa Ratten

LA Trobe University, Australia

As business landscape constantly shifts in today's digital age, this timely series looks at how business and society can harness technological innovation to succeed and drive progress. The books in this series identify new innovation capabilities and emerging technologies and investigate the managerial implications of such technologies. As business processes become increasingly complex, the series also explores how businesses can transform themselves with new digital technologies while aligning themselves with today's societal goals. This series provides direction through research on innovation and technology management and will be of benefit to anyone who is keen to thrive in an evolving business environment.

A Global Guide to FinTech and Future Payment Trends
Peter Goldfinch

For more information about this series, please visit www.routledge.com/Innovation-and-Technology-Horizons/book-series/ITH

A GLOBAL GUIDE TO FINTECH AND FUTURE PAYMENT TRENDS

Peter Goldfinch

Routledge
Taylor & Francis Group

LONDON AND NEW YORK

First published 2019
by Routledge
2 Park Square, Milton Park, Abingdon, Oxon OX14 4RN

and by Routledge
52 Vanderbilt Avenue, New York, NY 10017

Routledge is an imprint of the Taylor & Francis Group, an informa business

British Library Cataloguing-in-Publication Data
A catalogue record for this book is available from the British Library

Library of Congress Cataloging-in-Publication Data
Names: Goldfinch, Peter, author.
Title: A global guide to fintech and future payment trends /
Peter Goldfinch.
Description: 1 Edition. | New York : Routledge, 2019. | Includes
bibliographical references and index.
Identifiers: LCCN 2018040791 (print) | LCCN 2018047815 (ebook) |
ISBN 9780429401176 (ebook) | ISBN 9781138394452 (hardback) |
ISBN 9781138394469 (pbk.)
Subjects: LCSH: Payment. | Electronic funds transfers. | Credit cards. |
Debit cards.
Classification: LCC HG1692 (ebook) | LCC HG1692 .G65 2019 (print) |
DDC 332.1/78–dc23
LC record available at https://lccn.loc.gov/2018040791

ISBN: 978-1-138-39445-2 (hbk)
ISBN: 978-1-138-39446-9 (pbk)
ISBN: 978-0-429-40117-6 (ebk)

Typeset in Bembo
by Wearset Ltd, Boldon, Tyne and Wear

MIX
Paper from
responsible sources
FSC® C013056
www.fsc.org

Printed and bound in Great Britain by
TJ International Ltd, Padstow, Cornwall

CONTENTS

FIGURES

TABLES

ABBREVIATIONS

3DSecure	3 dimensional security system
ABA	Australian Banking Association
ABC	Australian Broadcasting Commission
ACH	Automatic Clearing House
AML	Anti-Money Laundering
ANZ Bank	Australian and New Zealand Bank
APCA	Australia Payment Clearing Association
API	Application Programming Interface
App	Application commonly used with reference to mobile
ARPU	Average Revenue Per Unit
ATM	Automatic Teller Machine
AUD	Australian Dollar
BACs	Bankers' Automated Clearing Services
BIN	Bank Identification Number
BIP	Buyer Initiated Payment
BPAY	Australian Bill Payment System
CAGR	Compounded Annual Growth Rate
CAPEX	Capital Expense
CB	Correspondent Bank
CGAP	Consultative Group to Assist the Poor
CNP	Card Not Present
CP	Card Present
CUP	China Union Pay
CVV1	Card Verification Value 1 and 2
DDA	Demand Deposit (bank) Account
EDC	Electronic Data Capture
EFTPOS	Electronic Funds Transfer at the Point of Sale
EMV	Europay, MasterCard and Visa, the original parties behind defining smart card standard

ESAS	Exchange Settlement Exchange System
EU	European Union
FEP	Front End Process
FSS	Faster Settlement Service
GBP	Great Britain Pound
GDPR	General Data Protection Regulation
GFC	Global Financial Crisis
GNI	Gross National Income
GSMA	Global System for Mobile Communications Association
HCE	Host Computer Emulation, host based mobile wallet
HSM	Hardware Security Module
IBAN	International Bank Account Number
ICL	International Computers Limited
ID	Identification
IFC	International Finance Corporation
IIN	Interbank Information Network
IOT	Internet of Things
IP	Internet Protocol
IRB	Indian Reserve Bank
ISO	International Standards Organization
IVR	Integrated Voice Response
KYC	Know Your Customer
MAC	Message Authentication Code
NFC	Near Field Communications
NGO	Non-Government Organization
NPP	National Payment Platform (Australia)
OPEX	Operating Expenses
P2B	Person-to-Business money transfer
P2P	Person-to-Person money transfer
P2PE	Point two Point Encryption
PAN	Primary Account Number
PBM	Personal Banking Machine
PC	Personal Computer
PCI	Payment Card Industry
PCI-DSS	Payment Card Industry – Data Security Standard
PCI PA-SSC	Payment Card Industry Payment Application Data Security Standard
PCI PTS	Payment Card Industry PIN Transaction Security
PCI-SSC	Payment Card Industry – Security Standards Council
PIN	Personal Identification Number
PKI	Public Key Infrastructure
POI	Point of Interaction
POS	Point of Sale
PSD2	Payment Services Directive 2

PSP	Payment System Processor
PTM	PC, Tablet and Mobile Phone platform
QR	Quick Response Code
RBA	Reserve Bank of Australia
RFP	Request For Proposal
ROI	Return on Investment
RTGS	Real-Time Gross Settlement
RTP	Real-Time Payment
SBRF	Savings Bank of Russian Federation
SEPA	Single Euro Payments Area
SKU	Stock Keeping Unit
SME	Small, Medium Size Enterprise
SWIFT	The global provider of secure financial messaging services
Swift MT	Swift Money Transfer
UK	United Kingdom
USA	United States of America
USSD	Unstructured Supplementary Service Data

1
INTRODUCTION

About the author

After five years of working for an organization owned by New Zealand's four major trading banks, being responsible for the all bank ATM and POS networks and the card management systems, both debit and credit, Peter, along with partners, established a consultancy and services partnership – GFG Group. Peter has developed an international footprint either as an individual or as a team leader completing assignments in over 30 markets. He has a balance of experience due to undertaking assignments in developed markets such as Australia, Japan, Hong Kong, Canada, United Kingdom and New Zealand as well as across emerging markets such as Iraq, Bangladesh and Vietnam plus equally challenging markets of India and the Philippines.

Peter has developed extensive business and technical knowledge from delivering payment solutions, many of which involved the delivery of transactional switching services. Peter has played key roles in significant projects such as the:

- first significant deployment of payment cards into the Russia (SBRF) market;
- initial design and business case for the Maldives interoperable payment system (National Payment System);
- Smart Communication's Smart Money (Philippines) mobile payment system – as the architect as well as project (integration) director;
- ISC's interoperable payments network in IRAQ;
- establishment of the Bahrain near real-time payment service.

Through these projects and many other assignments Peter truly demonstrates an understanding of the payments business, from system conception, design and development to implementation at both the business and technology levels. He understands the importance of transactional messaging systems (interoperability), the need for integrity in a payment service and the requirement to authenticate and secure payment data.

The content of this book is derived from this broad-ranging career in payments.

Who should read this book?

Peter has been asked over the years, by new entrants to the payment industry, how do I learn about payment systems? Are there courses or books that can be read? There are, and there are many opinion pieces and large amounts of content on the web, but most of it is topic specific and much opinion based.

This book is intended to address this gap. It is intended to be read by those entering the industry, such a technologists, business executives, and investors who are not interested in building a payment system, at least not immediately, but because of their careers or business interests require a level of understanding.

Because of the evolutionary nature of payments, this book looks from the past to the future so the reader can understand the industry dynamics. Not all readers will agree with Peter's projections for the future but it may help readers to define their own projections. If that happens an objective has been achieved.

Peter suspects payment systems are a difficult subject to comprehend, although people use payment services every day. As individuals or as participants in businesses, in small incremental steps, we determine which new technology-driven innovations will be successful.

This book is intended to assist the reader to navigate the payments landscape.

2

CONTEXT OF PAYMENTS

An understanding

Payment systems have changed dramatically over the last three to four decades, as electronic payments as a collective has become the dominant delivery mechanism. What was once solely a financial institution (bank) domain has broadened to where other parties have a major influence. Retailers have always been involved, but have become a strong lobby group, pressurizing the central monetary authorities to regulate to their advantage. Mobile operators have seen payments as an opportunity to extend their dominance, and with the encouragement of their own association (GSMA) and funding from various donor organizations, have attempted to enter the payments space, particularly in the emerging markets.

There has been the growth in third-party providers who have serviced the gaps in the market created because of the banks' preference not to provide a holistic service. Banks have looked to outsource or divest from various services, especially as the range of delivery channels has grown. Finally, the internet has been accepted as a legitimate platform from which to conduct commerce. The internet has presented the opportunity for services such as PayPal to enter the payments industry. We are seeing a variety of other organizations, which are not so easy to categorize, such as Google, Apple, Square and Amazon, becoming or attempting to become payment industry players.

In the last few years, Faster (Direct) Payment services have been introduced with the potential to challenge the card schemes and place pressure on cheques and cash usage. Although initially designed for the person-to-person market, the SME (small-, medium-size enterprise) sector is showing signs of being an early adopter. As the transaction limits are increased, corporate interest has increased beyond customer bill payments.

I sometimes think the payment industry (it was once only a sector of banking) is in a state of disorder (disruption) owing to the overwhelming attention from parties who believe they can make their fortune with minimal knowledge of the business, as revolutionaries supported by a superior understanding of how technology can be applied.

The disruption process results in a considerable amount of noise and wheel spinning, delivering slow progress at best. The reasons for this are possibly:

- The banks are considered conservative organizations, seen by many as slow to innovate. In part this is a fair comment and in some respects banks could claim this as a virtue considering they are custodians of our money. When they act otherwise we have outcomes such as the Global Financial Crisis (GFC). However, in the 1980s and 1990s, banks were innovators in the area of payments with the introduction of ATMs and POS (Point of Sale), extending the range of payment cards, telephone banking, and introducing cost saving technology in their back offices, etc. The reason banks have not been seen as innovators in recent years is the smart card and mobile-based technology solutions have not had the supporting business cases, with the associated risks having been assessed as too high. This is not to say banks have not taken to market their own internet-based solutions delivered across the PC, Tablet and mobile user platforms.

- Payments, as an industry, have attracted many technology-based solutions looking for a problem to solve. Smart cards are a primary example; NFC (Near Field Communications, i.e. mobile wallets) is looking like another. Many new payment initiatives are driven by technologists, with little understanding of the business and the associated market demands (I once placed myself in this category). Software solutions are often over-engineered, oversold and trying to address too many issues. Smart Cards are now will established, based on satisfying a core need. The need that had to be addressed was fraud. All the other financial services that were originally envisioned for Smart Cards having been forgotten, with mobile banking stealing the limelight. Proximity or contactless (tap and go) payment is also gaining traction, which indicates a bright future for NFC (at least on plastic).

- The retail industry, like the banks, is struggling with the technology options now available. Bricks and mortar retail outlets are being replaced with online sales channels. How retailers engage with their customers is currently a perplexing issue. Payment is part of the engagement equation, but how the payment industry responds will only be known once retailers settle on a new marketing and engagement model.

A new payment method must originate from one of the following:

- a new method of commerce being introduced such has been seen with the internet;

- a need to improve the efficiency of an existing payment method, such as cheques, cards and cash;
- a need to minimize the payment risk of an existing payment method as was the case for EMV (chip and PIN) over magnetic stripe and signature for cardholder validation;
- a customer's perceived need requiring fulfilment.

Are the emerging faster payment services the future? This is a question worth asking and it will be examined later.

To simplify the subject and to conceptualize, I see three interconnecting success factors that are core to any payment service (Figure 2.1).

~ In Figure 2.1, 'Trust' relates to security and confidentially of the payment process and safeguarding the identity of the payer; addressing fraud and preventing identity theft.

~ 'Friction' relates to the efficiency of the payment process, enabling it to be seamless in the purchasing experience. The new terminology is 'frictionless payments'.

~ The 'cost' of a payment transaction is always a contentious issue, but simply relates to volume. Consumer payments are a numbers game. As volume goes up cost should diminish simply through the economies of scale that are being achieved.

A payment method that delivers on the first two elements has a high possibility of achieving the third through the support of the payment participants.

Payment is the activity or process that supports (or enables) commerce. It is not the 'main act' but if payment cannot be made the commercial process will fail.

Figure 2.2 illustrates the steps related to making a purchase and the positioning of payment in the process.

Obviously, the duration of each step relates to the type of product and service being purchased, and in the case of supermarket shopping you might make several purchases but only one payment. You might argue there is no negotiation, but you might select a brand/product based on the price and quality.

FIGURE 2.1   Payment system success factors

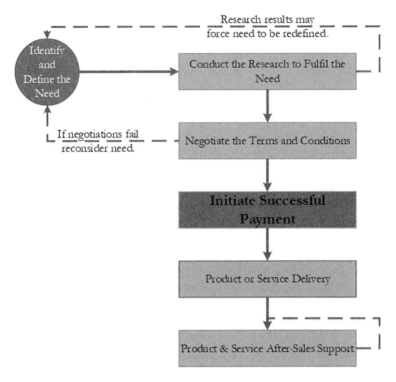

Research results may force need to be redefined.

Identify and Define the Need

Conduct the Research to Fulfil the Need

If negotiations fail reconsider need

Negotiate the Terms and Conditions

Initiate Successful Payment

Product or Service Delivery

Product & Service After-Sales Support

FIGURE 2.2 Purchasing chain

The biggest change in commerce has come from the emergence of the internet and e-commerce. E-commerce could be argued as the internet enabling mail order and catalogue sales channels to broaden their target market. The payment providers, especially the card schemes were late in recognizing that the front-end payment process needed to be re-engineered, so PayPal and similar services moved into the space. This should be a lesson to the established providers – adapt quickly or miss out.

Why is a payment system so important?

The payment system is a critical component of a national economy. Commence is severely inhibited if an efficient supporting payment system has not been deployed.

An excellent analogy is to compare the payment system to a nation's transportation network. Roads, rail and air networks allow goods to be transported from the points of production to their point of distribution and then through the delivery channels to the end user (customer).

Poor or non-existent transportation links restrict economic development. Producers need to deliver their products to market. Modern transportation links enlarge the market place for producers. This enables producers to increase their output, achieve greater economies of scale, and reduce their costs to enable them to be more competitive. Obviously poor transportation links reverses the situation, restricting the producer's market and their ability to grow their business.

The payment system is as critical as the transportation network. To support producers there is the need for an efficient payment system. Receipt of payment through the distribution chain allows producers to fund their businesses. This is most important for SMEs and sole traders, including primary producers who do not necessarily have access to the working capital available to larger businesses. Accessing loans to cover short-term funding requirements is often not an option, regardless of whether the business is operating in a developed or emerging economy.

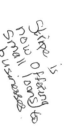 *fine offering is now Small loans to businesses*

An instruction to make an electronic payment generates a number of messages that flow down communication links to switches that reroute the messages either to another switch or to the final destination, which in most cases is a bank. The response will be returned most likely but not necessarily down the same route to the originator of the instruction.

This is very similar to a truck delivering a product from a warehouse to a retail outlet. The only real difference is one takes milliseconds, the other possibly hours if not days. One is electronic, the other physical.

Payment networks have the same problem with congestion that occurs on transport links. At certain times volume will increase well above the norm. Both networks have to be developed to handle the peaks. So therefore the planning processes for both are very similar.

This became apparent to me when I was introduced to a business in the south west of London whose prime source of income was modelling truck deliver routes for supermarket chains to maximize the efficiency of their networks. When I visited the business, they had just closed out a contract to use their technology and knowledge to model payment messages for a central bank to achieve the same outcome.

The point being made is a country's payment infrastructure is as critical to its economic development as other infrastructure components of the economy. There is no point improving levels of productivity and shipping of output to market if there is not an efficient and trustworthy payment system to ensure producers/manufacturers are being paid in a timely manner.

Transport networks require a set of rules and controls to be in place to ensure traffic flows and accidents are kept to a minimum. The payment system of any country demands the same disciplines.

There have been a number of payment projects in developing markets, funded by NGOs and development organizations targeting a specific need without taking a wider view. Some short-term gain is often made but mass-market adoption fails to eventuate. The primary reason is these new payment services are not being built in a manner that supports integration into a broader payment network. The Indian Reserve Bank has shown a considerable amount of leadership to drive the development of an affordable payment system into rural regions. Vietnam is another country also developing in a coherent manner. The Central Banks of Iran and Iraq both have the view that a national network compliant to international standards must be deployed. However, the norm has been to see disparate systems being implemented but where there is little consideration for interoperability, especially domestically and, equally importantly, internationally.

Many may point the finger at East Africa; I would point the finger at the mobile payment sector in general.

Future projections

I am a believer in not being afraid of voicing ones views and therefore subjecting one's own creditability to scrutiny. As strategists we need to have well-reasoned and developed projections of the future. For payments with so much noise being made by the FinTech self-appointed experts it is important to develop a rational future view.

I am not afraid to be proven wrong, although I would say in most cases it is the timing I get wrong not the outcomes. We are all overly optimistic in this industry. Therefore, I have 12 projections (see Table 2.1) that will be delivered over the next 15 years. I would prefer to say 10 years but it will probably be 20 years, so 15 is a compromise.

I have the long-term dream that one day we will simply only need to look at a device with a camera and microphone and simply say 'pay by ....'. The device, using facial image and voice recognition technology will identify and validate the payer, linking them to their bank account for authorization and debiting of their balance.

The payer does not need a card, a mobile wallet, or something wearable so this will reduce the cost. There is little friction and it is secure if biometric (two factors) technology is deployed. A third factor such as an iris scan could be added.

If account selection was a requirement, the system could ask for account type or if your default is your current account but you wanted to use your credit account then the initial instruction could be extended to 'pay credit'.

I could leave both my wallet and my mobile (which is becoming larger) at home.

Between writing the above and publication I had the opportunity to spend time with a FinTech group who had developed a biometric recognition solution. The problem was not the technology but a lack of understanding of where their solution would fit within the payment eco-system. Their technology has the potential for integration with the existing payment processes, playing a role in countering identity fraud. However, for broad-based acceptance, development of industry standards is a prerequisite.

Transition phase

There is a case to argue that payment systems are in a transactional phase, resulting in a period where there are more services than is needed. The older services are hanging on supported by those unwilling to adapt to change. Rationalization and modernization is needed.

The individual elements in Figure 2.3 are covered in this book and their positioning will be become obvious. The overall point that should be made as

TABLE 2.1 Future projections

No.	Description	Supporting comments
1	Cheques (or Checks) will be phased out in all countries, with the exception of perhaps the USA.	The UK has already attempted to do this but charities objected because a significant percentage of their donations are made by cheque.
		Cheques are a hangover from the pre-electronic age. Individual cheques originally needed to be returned for presentation at the branch of the payer to be cleared. Although banks have changed their operational model with truncation and imaging being introduced, a cheque remains a cheque and has no place in a world of electronic real-time payments.
		Simply costly with a high level of friction.
2	Cash usage will decline but never totally disappear, leading to ATMs not being replaced in non-strategic locations.	Cash supports the grey economy. This economy is less about criminal behaviour but a desire to reduce one's tax burden.
		Cash usage seems to increase in times of economic recession. I will stay away from the politics but if you have higher taxes and a recession then it's a perfect storm for those that support the longevity of cash as a payment instrument.
		In simple terms, its usage will fluctuate but the usage will continue a downwards trend, at an increasing rate.
3	Credit and debit cards will evolve into a single payment instrument.	Financial institutions will pull the traditional evolving credit account type into its retail bank domain and deliver more innovative credit products, still supported by a card, maybe.
		Credit card processing carries the legacy, like cheques, of originating from the pre-electronic age.
		Credit cards were like no other banking product; when initially introduced the concept of unsecured lending was counter to bankers' DNA.
		One banker told me that staff considered misfits were transferred to the credit card department.
		Further the original processes were paper-based and have essentially been maintained in an electronic form with virtually no re-engineering.

continued

TABLE 2.1 Continued

No.	Description	Supporting comments
4	Identity theft will be the primary mechanism used by fraudsters.	This will specifically be linked to the Internet of Things where we are connected to a network regardless of the device type, protected by a slim layer of security in most cases.
5	Because of fraud (above), mobile phone security will become a focus relating to identity theft. Financial institutions will become engaged with mobile phone vendors in introducing mechanisms to address this threat.	Mobile phones are becoming our personal mobile bank branch. Phones may well need to be partitioned so the banking and payment services operate separately to other mobile functions, in their own secured domain. Biometrics has been around for a long time with few takers, especially within the developed economies. Expect this to change and be core to the mobile authentication process.
6	Real-time payments (RTP) will become the dominant payment service replacing many of the traditional payment methods, especially those with a paper and batch history.	The payment methods affected will be the cheque as well the direct credit and debit services. Card transactions are also likely to be impacted but how is a little unclear. With the usage of debit cards increasing significantly we must see change. The plastic card may disappear for a virtual card, again linked to a biometric profile. QR codes are an option, maybe in the manner deployed by Alipay.
7	Because of RTP, it is expected that clearinghouse volumes will flatten out, if not decline.	There is a dependency on the larger billers and credit payment originators (such as governments and welfare services) to re-engineer their systems. Large volume will continue to be conveniently handled in bulk (maybe not as batch files) so this projection is tempered.
8	Retail payments well continue to strive to be more frictionless.	This is less a payment system concern, conditional on security not being compromised. Financial institutions will not drive this beyond their ability to support new methods of commerce. Merchants will have to drive this change, which is most likely to be delivered by PSPs.

9	Visa and MasterCard, and to a lesser extent American Express and Discovery, will find increased competition from schemes originating from India, China and Russia.	With the US administration using its control over international payment schemes to achieve political objectives, the world will seek out alternatives.
		This projection is not supporting a view that the USA's action is either appropriate or inappropriate. These alternative schemes already exist today to varying degrees. It is just something that is happening.
		China Union Pays' international subsidiary (UPI) appears to have a strategy of moving into the emerging markets as an issuer. It is also building up its image by supporting card acquiring in the markets where Chinese tourists are visiting. This provides a position to leverage in a longer-term game.
10	Crypto-currencies will be developed, but not as we know them.	This reminds me of Mondex. There are serious business and governance issues.
		The technology components (Blockchain) have an interesting and bright future.
		The reported constraint pertaining to transactions per second rates suggests this technology may only be used for niche payment services, and possible higher value payments.
11	Demise of the 'end of day'.	Traditionally, payments have revolved around an end-of-day clearing and settlement circle. Interim day settlement windows have been progressively introduced in many countries.
		With the implemented Australian NPP supporting transactions by transaction settlement for all payments, regardless of value, success should standardize this model.
		The RTGS system may be replaced by an Australian style Faster Settlement Service (FSS).
12	FinTech will run out of energy by 2025.	The FinTech phenomena will stall because of a low success rate and rising interest rates. Funds will go elsewhere.

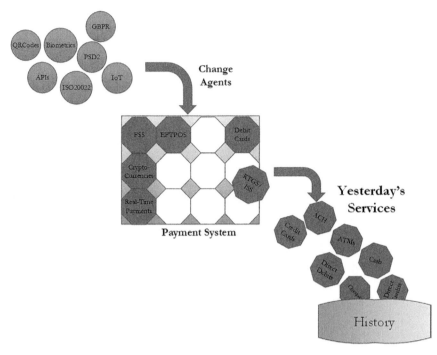

FIGURE 2.3   Payment system migrates from batch to real-time

Figure 2.3 illustrates the shift away from the physical to the virtual (or digital) and the shift to real-time. As will be mentioned throughout, the three factors of Trust, Friction and Cost are the underpinning elements.

Figure 2.3 also illustrates a rationalization of this current duplication of services as the physical services are phased out. With declining use, the cost to maintaining these services will become prohibitive. Service providers will not invest so expect service levels to decline, and fees will be increased or introduced to change behaviour.

With payment transactions migrating away from batch-style processing to real-time or near real-time processing, the business model for financial institutions, (inclusive of banks) is shifting away from the traditional silo model, where specific accounts and delivery channels were developed for a single service. This occurred organically rather than as a defined strategy because there was no clear road map of where technology would take commerce, banking and therefore payments. With a greater level of enlightenment, the banks working with business clients are in a position to develop and deploy more modular systems that can be easily integrated to deliver new or enhanced services.

3

DISRUPTION AND FINTECH

Electronic payments – early phase of disruption

Electronic payments began with the computerization of banking, a fact that cannot be in dispute. However, the two big steps that started the electronic payment revolution was the transformation of the T & E (travel and expenses) card into a broad based consumer credit/charge card and the introduction of ATMs.

ATMs should be rated as the most significant development as this was the first mass self-service electronic delivery channel. ATM networks were established by banks to pull customers out of branches, as they thought this would be more cost effective. It was believed that the first to develop their networks would gain a strategic advantage over their competitors. There is an argument that the substitution of four to five ATM transactions for each teller cash withdrawal did not deliver any cost savings. Bank customers would visit an ATM more frequently than a branch simply because it was more convenient. Further, not too many banks realized any competitor advantage as ATMs, when introduced into a market, quickly became a must-have service and all banks in various ways responded.

For more on ATMs see 'Where Electronic Payments Started – ATMS' in Chapter 5.

The credit card business and processing models progressively adopted technology. This process has not stopped. As an example, OCR (Optical Character Recognition) was introduced to read credit card vouchers, and was then replaced by EDC (Electronic Draft Capture) to improve efficiency by eliminating paper. Later, EDC was upgraded to EFTPOS (Electronic Funds Transfer at Point of Sale) for security reasons, inclusive of EMV, and now we have NFC and mobile phones playing a role.

For more on EFTPOS see the section in Chapter 5 entitled 'Point of Sale (EFTPOS or POS)'.

Banks today, regardless of the classification of their market, are managing an increasingly complex technology infrastructure supporting a broad range of payment services. Payment systems generally do not die but simply, to varying degrees, fade away. Cheques are still being used in significant numbers in many countries. Credit card vouchers are on rare occasions still used. Even telephone banking (IVR – Interactive Voice Response) in the age of mobile banking is surviving.

Banks need to answer the following questions.

- How do they maximize their return on existing investment when there is a continuing demand, (more often from the technologist) to introduce a new replacement service?
- The original investment in electronic payments was justified on the back of increased efficiency. If this is no longer necessarily valid, how do banks justify their investment in new technologies?
- How do banks react to non-industry players trying to secure a piece of the market?
- How do banks respond to pressure from governments and regulators to service an unprofitable market segment?

What we are seeing across many markets is that banks are demonstrating, to varying degrees, a willingness to withdraw from payment services by supporting third-party payment service providers in various disguises.

Many will claim this is evidence that banks are losing out to payment service providers. I would claim banks are strategically withdrawing, recognizing others can undertake the processing more efficiently. Banks' primary concern is to retain the customer relationship. They recognize others can undertake the heavy lifting (processing of high volume transactions) while they concentrate on the more strategic aspects of their core business, where they have the ability to maximize their profit.

Influence of technologists

The evolution of payments may be seen by many as technology driven but the pace has always been driven by the users (payers, consumers, merchants, payees) as well as by the financial institutions and service providers' appreciation of the users' propensity to accept progressive change.

It has not been considered a disruptive process (although it was) but as progress or social development. In earlier years the focus was on the back office, involving the building of systems that processed masses of data, generally in batches. These systems are frequently now referred to as legacy systems. Legacy systems, specifically in banking, laid a foundation for the development of a more interactive environment.

Has the interactive environment been impeded from reaching its full potential? ATM and point of sale services had been successfully introduced. Telephone banking services had been deployed and mobile text messaging had been discovered. For those of us in the payments industry we felt there was more.

So what has been the most significant game changer? The introduction of the Smartphone arguably began with the 'Internet of Things' (IoT). One of the issues with smart cards was they did not have a screen, keyboard or the ability to directly communicate. The mobile Feature Phone, as we now refer to them, addressed all of these issues but still I was not initially satisfied. I commented, when involved in the development of Smart Money in the Philippines (2000–2001) that mobile phones were like the IBM3624 ATM, tiny screen, numeric-only keyboard, limited memory and a restrictive telecommunications protocol. I had to go back in time with the architecting of mobile solutions on the Feature Phone until the arrival of the Smartphone. Smartphones have addressed these issues, and the user experience and service delivery capability is similar across PCs, Tablets and Mobile (Smart) Phones, (the PTM platform). Devices such as ATMs, or self-service devices, which have a PC under their hood (inside), have been given an extended future through the adoption of IoT.

The pedantic will point out that only Smartphones have wallets to support NFC. This is correct, but the wallet as a repository of payment instruments, loyalty memberships, etc., if based on HCE (Host Computer Emulation) can be managed and used by all three devices. We have not seen the end of the integration of the PTM platform.

Why the excitement?

Payments, as already mentioned, are driven by the user's willingness to adopt. Technologists will continue to develop innovative solutions to meet their perception of the users' needs. As technologists we repeatedly get it wrong. So it is import to understand what drives changes in user behaviour. To quote from the Edgar Dunn & Company, 11th Advanced Payments Report 2017:

> It is important to distinguish between consumer expectations and consumer needs. Consumer trends in the payments space typically are not driven by what consumers expect but by what they need. Consumer habits are hard to change. Consumers will not switch from a familiar method of payment to something new unless it is advantageous for them such as greater ease of use, enhanced security or cheaper price.

See Figure 2.1 and the success factors; trust, friction and cost!

Consumer practices have evolved over the last one to two decades, resulting in the emergence and growth in acceptance of e-commerce and internet banking services. Banks have pushed their customer-facing services out of branches into the homes, offices and the pockets of their customers – and their customers have generally responded – whereas ATMs only pulled a limited range of services onto the streets.

With this increase and broader use of electronic activity the fraudster community (or is fraud an industry?), has flourished. Fraudster ingenuity and technical capabilities have developed to keep pace with the opportunities presented by the adoption of payment technology.

For the card-present transactions, fraud finally delivered a business case (outside of the prepaid/stored value sector) for smart cards and the introduction of EMV. EMV has delivered a decline in card-present fraud.

The *Fraud The Facts 2016* Report, from Financial Fraud Action (FFA) UK, confirms for the moment that EMV has been effective with fraudsters switching their focus to card-not-present (CNP) transactions. CNP fraud has yet to be addressed, successfully. The European Central Bank *Fourth Report on Card Fraud* details the same story, although this report is dated July 2015.

This European Central Bank report stated that, for Europe in 2013, card-not-present fraud was 66 per cent of total card fraud. For Australia it was 72 per cent and Canada 61 per cent.

In the UK, the FFA places the cost, in 2014, of what it referred to as fraud in 'remote purchases' (internet, telephone and mail order) at 70 per cent of the total card fraud compared with 54 per cent in 2007. Online fraud against UK retailers was estimated at GBP189.4 million in 2016, a 20 per cent increase on the previous year.

The card industry has introduced 3D secure, CVV2 and tokenization to reduce fraud, which has probably made some impact, along with more sophisticated risk assessment technology. PCI data security (a set of rules and processes) has rightfully been enforced on the industry to address identified weaknesses.

Is the 'request and response' (card) model inherently weak? Are all these measures just an indication that the payment model is on 'life support'? The need to use increasingly more sophisticated risk assessment solutions, such as neural technology and extended PCI measures, produces costly solutions to plugging holes that should not exist. Is it time to throw out the model for CNP payments and introduce one without the inherent flaws?

We cannot expect cards to disappear as a payment instrument, whether the form factor is a piece of plastic with a chip or a mobile phone, or a wristband, or whatever the latest gadget. As stated before, payment instruments never die, they just fade away – consider cheques. Card payment participants have and continue to invest in the current card payment service and the market penetration is enormous. It simply cannot be replaced quickly.

It could be suggested that under EMV, at least for the meantime, the card-present payment holes have been plugged. The providers, therefore, have no urgency to change. Cardholders, however, may have another view based on cost, specifically surcharging, which many claim is the passing on of interchange fees, with a margin. However, the regulators may have seen the errors of their ways and surcharging may become disallowed in specific markets. The card schemes' opposition to surcharging, in my view, was always justified.

Consumers/businesses will decide

The payment specialist and technologists have this naïve view they will drive the future direction of payments. All technologists can do is put forward alternatives, and users will select.

The UK Faster Payment service has delivered annual growth for the years 2015–2017 for Standing Orders of 4 to 5 per cent, Single Immediate 20 to 21 per cent and Forward Dated 6 to 8 per cent. For 2016, in excess of 1400 million transactions were processed, with 62 per cent attributed to Single Immediate Payments. This represents 13+ transactions per person for the year.

Where are the Faster Payments coming from? UK Inter-Bank & Inter-Branch Transactions increased by only 3 per cent in 2016. The payment category that took the biggest hit was Cheque & Credit Clearing at minus 15 per cent for the same period (these statistics are published on UK Faster Payment website, www.faster-payments.org.uk).

A conclusion may be drawn that Faster Payments have yet to impact card payments. Card transaction numbers in the UK are not in a free fall but the growth rate looks to be on the decline. Refer to the UK Cards Association summary of key statistics (*Facts and Figures* – www.theukcardsassociation.org.uk/facts_figures/index.asp).

UK Faster Payments is a pay-away service referred to as Real-Time Payments (RTPs).

To quote the Edgar Dunn 11th Advanced Payments Report 2017:

> In contrast to the ACH or cards rails that have evolved their capabilities over time, today's RTP rails are designed to meet current requirements and be better prepared to address future needs. They match or improve on the functionality, security, and user experience provided by any of the other rails and with the advantage of having lower per transaction processing costs.

FinTech opportunity

The growth of internet-enabled devices and channels – the PTM platform (such as PCs, Tablets and Mobile (Smart) Phones) – has encouraged greater interest from non-traditional participants to enter the payments industry.

Many would suggest these new entrants are filling a void or meeting a customer need neglected by the banks. This argument has some merit, as banks are generally hesitant to embrace new technology until there is a proven business case. Using today's terminology, the FinTech (the term may be new but the activity is not) sector has for nearly three decades produced technology solutions looking for problems (customer needs) and a business case. However, taking a risk and venturing into the unknown is not the only way to discover the market acceptance level for a new approach to delivering an existing service.

Technologists need to rate their proposed payment services against the three factors of friction, trust and cost. They need to understand the proposition for each participant category in the payment chain, especially the users.

Chip cards are the prime example of a technology that promised so much but delivered so little. It may be argued that card fraud was required to reach a significant level before the business case materialized. The card industry has always suffered (as have other payment services, such as cash and cheques) from a fraud issue, but it was not until the problem in business terms reach a level requiring action that a solution needed to be found. When that happened, the solution was the 'chip'.

It could be argued if the UK had introduced the PIN with magnetic stripe as its colonial siblings had done, then chip and PIN would not have happened quite so quickly. But then parents rarely take advice from their children. Recently, when I visited the UK, I still needed to sign even though my card has a chip. As I do in France, but not Italy. I assume this is because the UK and France and many other countries cannot support PIN validation at '(issuer's) host'.

EMV cards essentially provided the cardholders with a heightened feeling of security, assuming they know what EMV accomplishes for them. In countries where PIN and magnetic stripe was established, the shift to EMV did not impact cardholders apart from inserting rather than swiping.

Chip cards are not so one-dimensional. Proximity cards or contactless or NFC (depending on your education) enabled cards introduced efficiencies at the point of acceptance (EFTPOS) to meet a retailer demand for frictionless payments. This tap and go service commercialized by the card schemes is based on no PIN being required for low value transactions, allowing their cards to be more broadly accepted, such as for mass transit. Even if a PIN is required, the speed of a tap and go, compared with inserting a card, is in my view far greater. I personally get annoyed if a retailer does not support contactless payments.

NFC has allowed the card form factor to be moved from plastic to the mobile smartphone, which has given birth to the mobile wallet. As a user of a mobile wallet I would argue that the frictionless aspect has not yet been significantly improved. The plastic form factor in many acceptance situations still wins out, but it might only be a question of the mobile wallet service maturing with a little fine tuning, leading to greater adoption.

This subject is explored later in this book, in Chapter 5, in the section entitled 'The Mobile Wallet'.

The internet or card-not-present (CNP) payment market provided PayPal with the opportunity to become a significant international payment service provider. Services such as PayPal provide a 'wall' in part protecting the banks from the risks. I do not see PayPal as a competitor of the banks or card issuers but as a provider of a complementary service. One the card schemes should have provided.

Payment services using social media as a channel have significant potential. Social media connects people so using these services for peer-to-peer money transfers must gain user acceptance. The Chinese service WeChat is an example.

An underlying issue for the payments industry with regard to CNP payments has been the authentication of the person initiating a payment to determine their rights to the funds being accessed. The card associations have attempted to address this with a range of security and risk mitigation programs including the promotion of prepaid cards.

Sophisticated risk management solutions (systems and services) have been developed. These solutions, although minimizing the risk are not addressing the core problem. This approach is common for the payments industry where often the business is only concerned with maintaining the risk within affordable limits rather than investing in technology or changing business practices to remove the risk, which comes at a greater cost. This is the process of normalization where all parties are happy to live with the risk, as long as controls or constraints are in place.

FinTech frustration

FinTech participants do find their position frustrating, believing they can deliver technology solutions that are demanded by consumers and business – solutions that they consider will address existing inefficiencies and deliver cost savings.

I recently purchased a physical book at an airport, which in itself is now a rare event. With eight flying hours ahead, reading this book was a better option than watching endless movies. The book was *The Fintech Book, The Financial Technology Handbook for Investors, Entrepreneurs and Visionaries*, edited by Susanne Chishti and Janos Barbers, published by Wiley in 2016. The book is a compilation of a number of opinion pieces written by a range of authors. I recommend this book for a number of reasons, as it provides an insight into the mindset of the FinTech fraternity, their enthusiasm, and often great thinking (but some of is a little woolly).

The book's coverage is far broader than payments, but I read it with my payment blinkers on.

Without identifying specific authors, the following points need to be challenged:

- Banks are no longer trusted and technology companies are more trusted.
- Technology companies can deliver services at a lower cost.
- Banks have a considerable amount of data they are not using and should make available to those that can use and monetarize.

I would accept that banks are probably, as a generalization, less trusted than a decade ago due to their behaviour leading to the GFC. However, in the payment space, I believe they are still trusted and far more than are technology companies. The need for PCI is based on PSPs and companies that hold payment details without providing adequate protection.

Cost is an interesting issue and it should not be confused with fees, which should be viewed as the price. Payment transaction processing costs are driven by volume. High volume translates to low per transaction cost. There are a number of costs related to support services and regulatory compliance. The card scheme list of charges seems to be never ending and on top of these must be added the issuers' and acquirers' own costs.

Banks hold a considerable amount of data on their customers but has it value? Banks only know their customers' spending behaviour relating to the accounts they manage. They know who their customers are paying but not what they are buying. The merchant category code will indicate in broad terms what a merchant is selling. Banks will know how much is being spent at a specific supermarket but will not know, for example, if the customer is vegetarian or an excessive red meat consumer. For more discussion refer to the later section in this chapter on 'Big data'.

The 2017 *World Payments Report* by Capgemini & BNP Paribas, covers a survey that shows that, for the FinTech sector, the banks' agility to adapt to new ways is a big issue. Banks conversely find data privacy and cybersecurity to be their biggest concerns, with also one third of the respondents concerned about the lack of clarity on regulatory specifics.

I find this last point to be the biggest issue and it does relate back to the banks' other two concerns. It is easy for regulators to capitulate to lobby groups on their demands without being too concerned about the consequences, treating these as mere implementation issues for the banks to address. Elements of PSD2 illustrate this point. The Australian changes back in the early 2000s are another case, especially concerning surcharging.

FinTech participants recognize that banks have an agility challenge and recognize that banks have constraints relating to regulation. These regulations will increasingly impact the FinTech sector, which itself will become less agile.

Banks or financial institutions will not adopt a new technology unless there is a benefit in terms of reduced cost or the delivery of a strong competitive advantage that is underpinned by a strong customer demand.

A key point for technologists to understand is that payment services are not a financial institution's core business. It would be rare to find a financial institution making significant profits from payments (excluding interest on credit cards). Banks make profits from the interest rate spread between the cost of funds and their lending/investment portfolio revenues.

The Capgemini & BNP Paribas report suggests banks are moving away from the traditional view that payment is a non-core business. I am not quite convinced this is the case. Yes, we are seeing new technology advances with respect to the user interfaces, but what is the motivation? It is reducing cost through introducing more efficient processes plus the need to deal with fraud or competitive pressure.

There is the suggestion that banks should work on the integration of payment data with the pools of non-payment big data sources to assist their clients. This would involve working with other banks, the FinTech sector, and their chosen third party development partners. This would allow banks to deliver value added services to their business and corporate clients. Who owns the data, banks or their customers? PSD2 answers this question.

What will become critical to banks is their ability to meet the interests of both their retail clients and business clients, but whose interests could be diametrically opposed to each other. The FinTech sector in the *The Fintech Book* criticizes banks for not servicing the business sector. I believe this is not the case as banks with a focus on this sector will have business account managers and, for the larger businesses and corporations, account teams. This is the sector where banks make real money.

Without doubt and we are seeing banks working with the FinTech sector on the development of innovative solutions. The question is, will the FinTech sector be mature enough to accept it is the junior partner in such a relationship? The banks own the end user relationship and FinTech partners need to understand this factor to ensure success.

So many have never spent so much on failure

All of us who have been in this industry for an extended time have seen an enormous amount of technology-based development, much of which has failed to deliver on the expectations of developers/investors. Smart Cards is a prime example, but mobile appears to be repeating history. Developers come in all sizes, from the technologists working off their mum's kitchen table to the large multinational with seemingly unlimited funds. Some can afford failure as long as one in 'x' is successful.

However, it is not all gloom at the macro level. The payment industry has progressed reasonably quickly. Probably as quickly as the average person, the user, can handle. It is also interesting that certain technologies take time to find the problem to solve; or the problem materializes to a point where action needs to be taken. EMV is probably an excellent example; however, I think biometrics is probably a better one.

A colleague tried to sell me on biometric authentication in the early 1990s, but it was almost 20 years later that I became involved in a project that had a biometric component. It was an Iraq client upgrading their service (supporting government benefit payments), transitioning to an EMV compliant card supporting fingerprint authentication for domestic acceptance. That was at the same time that India and the Philippines were also initiating projects for government ID cards supported by biometrics. My passport now supports facial recognition. My mobile phone supports fingerprint biometric as an alternative to a password, but not very well. My bank recently requested that they take a voiceprint for customer authentication and it works. Far better than answering five questions that I always get wrong.

Why biometrics? It goes back to the three factors mentioned earlier, and biometrics addresses friction. Managing logons and passwords is one of the most annoying elements of modern life. Biometrics also protects the user's identity if deployed appropriately.

FinTech participants at fault

Back to today. The development of internet services, utilization of mobile technology as a payment delivery channel and the participation of an expanded array of participants has made payments a far more interesting industry. The drivers for the new non-bank entrants are not clear. A view is that existing services are too costly, and a market open to new entrants will deliver more efficient business models that will without doubt be embraced. Only a small percentage of the market needs to be captured to deliver a more than acceptable ROI. Seemingly a rational view, it rarely proves to be a winning view.

Of the FinTech sector it could be said, 'So many have never spent (or will spend) so much on failure'.

Many point the finger for such failure at the traditional market participants, specifically the banks and the card schemes. In fact, the reasons are more fundamental.

- Maturity of the technology such as with biometrics.
- Cost, not of the technology but to deploy it.
- Disruptive not only to the service provider but, importantly, to the user, with minimal perceived benefit.
- Timing is always critical especially if an alternative (even if inferior) solution has recently been deployed.
- Non-compliant to industry standards.

All and each of the above will deliver a poor business experience.

With chip and PIN, prior to tap and go, the end user proposition did not seem strong, but it was strong for the card issuers and schemes. Cardholders did accept this new technology with little resistance. Many were probably unware of the chip on their card but had been using PIN entry at ATMs. Introducing PINs at the point of sale may have seemed a natural and preferred approach over scribbling one's signature on a piece of paper. The point being, it is difficult to judge user acceptance.

Big data

On reading a number of papers, including the 2017 World Payments Report by Capgemini & BNP Paribas, I concluded there was considerable FinTech activity on the fringes of payments, but more outside of payments.

It will vary by country, by region, but payment messages rarely carry SKU (Stock Keeping Unit) data (if compliant to ISO8583), and in-store ECR systems do not capture payment details. This means that the PSPs and banks know you have spent $X at a specific merchant but they have no data regarding the products/ services purchased. Retailers know they have made a sale and those with ECR/ ERP systems will know what has been sold but not to whom.

The 'whom' question is often resolved through loyalty programs. By customers signing up to a retailer's loyalty program and presenting their loyalty card at the time of purchase (to earn something), retailers are provided with an answer to the 'whom' question.

Multi retail loyalty programs can deliver analysis across their member's broader spending habits.

Another unsatisfactory situation for many retailers and manufactures/producers is not being able to link the activities of the purchasing process, as presented in Figure 2.2.

I once spent a few hours talking to a couple of very bright media people who were trying to solve this problem. When they ran an advertising campaign for a client they could measure the increased visits to the client's website but they could not determine how many went on to purchase the product.

If they knew the answer to this question they could change their media-pricing model to be results based.

If the payment messages support extended purchasing data (as ISO20022 can potentially deliver) by linking the purchasing activity across the purchasing chain the buyer could be identified. The issue is that the purchaser changes their unique identity factor as they pass through the chain. These identity factors being the IP address, email address, loyalty membership number and payment instrument (card or account) number. For a simple purchase it may simply be an IP address and payment instrument number.

To complicate the process, there are multiple card issuers, acquirers and various payment service providers who all hold some of the data but not all. The only solution is for an in-market data warehouse (utility) where everyone submits their data and has the rights to the collective whole. Using date and time, location, and so on, it might be feasible to link and consolidate all the pieces of data to answer the various questions of the marketers.

However, the question arises, who actually owns the data and do third parties have the right to use the data and make it available to all. Privacy becomes a big issue.

It is a confusing situation, with too many pieces to the jigsaw puzzle to allow for the building of individual customer profiles. Retailers, online or in-store should at least be able to identify customers and know their purchasing history, perhaps going back to the old fashioned art of person-to-person selling in order to build interpersonal relationships. I am not sure how you emulate that online.

A further issue in this space is why would retailers share SKU data with other retailers? The anecdotal evidence in Australia is that six retailer groups own 80 per cent of the retail trade. Enriching the data in a payment message is potentially giving away a competitive advantage. Entering into bilateral arrangements with non-competitive groups in the club of six may deliver a better result and, as mentioned above, can be achieved through loyalty programs. This is not a 100 per cent solution.

Direct payments – near real-time payment services

There is quite a revolution starting to pick-up momentum within the Direct Payments sector. Traditionally this sector has been less than glamorous because it covers the process of clearing cheques, direct credits and debits, standing orders, automatic or re-occurring payments. Further, it has an end-of-day batch processing orientation.

New near real-time or faster payment services are beginning to emerge, led initially by the United Kingdom but now also being supporting by the European Central Bank and PSD2. These services are based on the 'pay away' method where the payer requests their financial institution to make a payment to a nominated payee.

While the mobile industry has been viewing payments from either a remittance or card prospective and becoming all excited by mobile wallets, the traditional payment participants are about to move not only the goal posts but also the playing field.

This new playing field is based on:

- smartphone technology using applications developed by the banks and their service providers;
- non-repudiated payments where cleared funds are available to the payee within seconds;
- a new standard, ISO20022, to enable more enriched data to be captured and forwarded with messages;
- initially domestic and EU regions supporting a single currency but medium-term cross-border will be brought into play.

If the momentum sustains itself it could change the payment industry significantly and threaten the status quo. Payment transactions to be most affected will be P2P and P2B.

This subject is explored in Chapter 5 under the heading 'Real-Time Payments'.

Cryptocurrencies and blockchain

A contemporary topic is cryptocurrencies with the payment services being supported by a blockchain platform.

In a sense, a cryptocurrency takes those of us who have become cashless back to a currency that is not physical but is identifiable. To explain, bank notes (fiat currency) have unique numbers so they can be traced, and identified as probably being genuine or counterfeit. They used to catch bank robbers when the stolen notes appeared in circulation, by tracing where they were presented. Cryptocurrency in an electronic form is similar, with a crypto value as the unique identify. A bitcoin once in circulation may have multiple owners but its identity does not change. Electronic money that we have become familiar with has no identity and no permanence, as it is just added to an existing account balance. Tracing can only be done from mapping messages.

I believe there is a need for a global currency that is not controlled by one country's regulatory authority. Many companies with international markets, especially from smaller countries, default to US$ as the currency to do business. With the controls and the scrutiny on international money transfers by the US authorities and the consequent transfer delays, an alternative is needed. Based on personal experiences the euro appears to becoming an alternative, but is also not perfect.

Cost and timeframe associated with international money transfers are also factors used by the supporters of cryptocurrencies. Again, based on personal experience, these two factors seem to be reducing. Somebody is listening, especially if the US authorities are not involved.

A paper published by Satoshi Nakamoto, the founder(s) of Bitcoin, entitled 'Bitcoin: A Peer-to-Peer Electronic Cash System', https://bitcoin.org/bitcoin.pdf, makes the following claim:

> We have proposed a system for electronic transactions without relying on trust. We started with the usual framework of coins made from digital signatures, which provides strong control of ownership, but is incomplete without a way to prevent double-spending. To solve this, we proposed a peer-to-peer network using proof-of-work to record a public history of transactions that quickly becomes computationally impractical for an attacker to change if honest nodes control a majority of CPU power. The network is robust in its unstructured simplicity. Nodes work all at once with little coordination. They do not need to be identified, since messages are not routed to any particular place and only need to be delivered on a best effort basis. Nodes can leave and rejoin the network at will, accepting the proof-of-work chain as proof of what happened while they were gone.

There is always a trust element. With fiat currencies we do trust financial institutions (if not fully), whereas with Bitcoin we are expected to trust technology. Technology solutions/systems are the creation of humans, and I suspect most people have had more than one negative technology experience.

If cryptocurrencies become broadly used then the payment rails built on blockchain will need to be integrated into the various payment delivery channels. How this is achieved will need to be developed but coexistence (interoperability) will be necessary.

China payment markets

Many see China as the powerhouse of payments and CUP (China Union Pay) and Alipay will dominate internationally. This should be viewed in context of how this country of 1.42 billion or 1.01 billion between the ages of 15 and 64 years (UN 2018 projection – see https://data.worldbank.org) compares with the rest of the world. As with the other tables in this book, we use the United Kingdom and Australia as benchmarks. Table 3.1 is extracted from The World Bank Financial Inclusion Data/Clobal FINDEX and the CIA WorldFact Book – see http://datatopics.worldbank.org/financialinclusion/ and www.cia.gov/library/publications/the-world-factbook/geos/uk.html.

TABLE 3.1 Key inclusion indicators – China comparison

Key inclusion indicators – China comparison	China	United Kingdom	Australia
Mobile subscribers per 100 inhabitants	99	122	114
Internet users (%)	53.2	94.8	88.2
Age 15–54 years (%)	61.29	52.45	54.24
Account ownership (banked indicator) (%)	88	98	100

These indicators, with the exception of internet users, place China on a par with the United Kingdom and Australia. The Account Ownership is at a lower percentage but not dramatically lower.

'Internet users' is the figure of significance in this age of IoT. This suggests that mobile is the dominant interactive channel.

Table 3.2 is a little more interesting, and is also extracted from World Bank Financial Data Global FINDEX figures. However, it is a little out of date being for 2014.

Table 3.2 clearly shows a comparative difference between China and the other two countries.

What is clear in these two sets of statistics is that China's internet penetration is low compared to mobile. These figures also tell us that China is about 50 per cent carded and that its payment channels are generating very low transaction volume.

It is still obviously a cash economy with a low per capita GNI. The ATM usage percentage is similar to the number of those who have a bank account. It could be assumed that money held in accounts is accessed through ATMs. A negative is that only 17.7 per cent have received wages into a bank account. I also consider the United Kingdom and Australian percentages as being low. However, government payments especially for Australia (40.5 per cent) boost the number receiving funds into their accounts.

TABLE 3.2 Other indicators – China comparison

Other indicators – China comparison	China	United Kingdom	Australia
GNI per capital ($)	6,540	41,680	65,400
Has a debit card (%)	48.6	96.4	88.9
ATM is the main mode of withdrawal (%)	51.2	70.1 (2011)	68.5
Used account to receive wages (%)	17.7	51.5	55.6
Used account to receive government transfer (%)	9.5	18.7	40.5
Used a financial institution account to pay utility bill (%)	15.1	71.6	64.1
Use debit card (%)	17.3	91.8	82.5
Use credit card (%)	13.8	55.3	56.3
Use internet bill/pay bill (%)	19.2	77.8	68.2

Using very simple logic, the potential for generating electronic payments is severely impacted if funds do not flow into bank accounts either from earnings (wages) or from government.

Blockchain

Cryptocurrency is linked to, and created the interest in, Blockchain technology. Blockchain is essentially an enabling technology. Many are possibly viewing Blockchain as a solution (technology) looking for a problem. I have no doubt that Blockchain improves traceability and therefore the auditing capabilities, specifically in the financial sector, by delivering a more robust process. As a generalization I would see the security elements conceptually as an improvement but, in practice, the Blockchain concerns relate to privacy. Transparency as a feature is counter to the payment industry's direction, specifically considering PCI-DSS.

Further, Blockchain may be an exciting new addition to the technology 'toolbox' but how does it improve life for the end user?

Could Blockchain be used in the more conventional payment space?

This is currently happening: Banking Technology ~ banking tech.com reported (18 October 2017) 'that J P Morgan had launched Interbank Information Network (IIN) for processing of global payments utilizing Blockchain technology'.

The report quoted Emma Loftus, head of global payments and FX, JP Morgan Treasury Services:

> IIN will enhance the client experience, decreasing the amount of time – from weeks to hours – and costs associated with resolving payment delays.
>
> Two banks have joined the network, (Royal Bank of Canada and Australia & New Zealand Bank) and more are expected to join.

But there are apparent issues with blockchain due to the technology being still immature. It was conceived in 2008, and only in recent years deployed. Commentators are suggesting:

- Even in a closed or private network all the participants can see the database content.
- The serial nature of updating means the time to process a transaction is extended, with ten transaction per second considered the upper limit.
- Blockchain is referred to as gossip protocol, where each transaction that occurs globally, within a network, must be updated to each node.

From a payment prospective, the sensitive data, I assume, would continue to be protected through encryption and the deployment of techniques such as tokenization. The critical factor is the impact on response times, especially when transactions are at peak load. A paper published by Dr Arthur Gervais and Rami Khalil, entitled 'Revive: Rebalancing Off-Blockchain Payment Networks' states that, 'Bitcoin currently only supports 7 transactions per second'. They go on to say,

> The simple re-parameterization of key blockchain parameters (such as the block interval or block size), has been shown to not allow a transaction load beyond 10 transactions per second.

To overcome this limitation, 'off-chain' networks must be implemented so payments are processed free of the Blockchain constraints. Examples of these are Bitcoin's Lightening Network and Ethereum's Raiden Networks. The scalability is achieved by not relying on the blockchain until it is required.

Conceptually, 'off-chain' networks could be used to support 'retail' payment networks such as EFTPOS, ATMs and extending out to RTP with the settlement being performed 'on-chain'. Settlement is the area of interest. The traditional hub and spoke networks, such as Visa and MasterCard, as well as many proprietary networks, rely on a custodial third party holding funds or securities to ensure the settlement risk of failure is minimized. Net settlement is derived by the custodian's hub and participants funds are either debit or credited based on their settlement position.

Blockchain supports primarily transactions between two parties viewed by the payments industry as a bilateral relationship. Larger monolithic bilateral networks are often referred to, sarcastically, by many as 'bird nest architecture'. The settlement of bilateral networks would lend itself to blockchain where each pairing generates a payment to each other; a payment that is 'on-chain' and carries all the related security elements. The settlement process is underpinned by a smart contract to ensure it takes placed at a specific time and/or if one party reaches the exposure limit, or simply their negative settlement position reaches a predetermined limit that settlement is required to be successfully executed before further transactions can be processed, to minimize the risk.

For a hub and spoke architecture, the transaction pairing is logically between the 'custodian' and the network participant. Using Visa as an example, it is the custodian and their clients, either card issuers or acquirers, who are the participants. Each participant in such a network has no relationship with Visa's other clients. Visa would be able to deploy a blockchain settlement process.

An assignment I recently undertook involved creating the architecture for a national ATM/POS network, with TPS rates in excess of 2000, over a wide geographical area, where the telecommunications infrastructure didn't instil a high level of confidence. This type of situation may be a candidate for an off- and on-chain network.

Would blockchain be a better solution than a conventional software switch with potentially multiple nodes supported by an active/active database configuration to achieve the required availability of 99.99 per cent?

An EFT transaction with its multiple ISO8583 messages, each being a block and chained to form the total transaction, would seem to be the ideal application, supported by a distributed database. Messages are protected within a block, giving the transactions the highest level of integrity for reconciling settlement positions between participants as well as dealing with cardholder/merchant disputes.

Such as system, because of the TPS rates, would need to be off-chain with settlement on-chain.

On reading about Ethereum I became more inspired and excited about blockchain as a technology. My take is that Ethereum is less about the payment, although it supports a cryptocurrency, but more about the commercial process it supports. A specific article by Tyler Keenan (www.business2community.com/author/tyler-keenan), 'What is Ethereum', discusses smart contracts;

> Smart contracts don't simply record the terms of the deal, as with a paper contract, they also automatically verify when the terms of the deal have been satisfied and facilitate the transfer of any goods, content, or money associated with it.

In this context it is assumed that payment could be in a fiat currency. The chain simply records the payment or schedule of payments made based on the terms of the contract. I can see significant business and legal advantages in this type of application. The use of the blockchain technology in this context can be extended and it allows the positioning of the payment within the commercial context rather than viewing it as a standalone event. This is an exciting concept.

Going forward

Returning to my previously stated reservations, the proposition for blockchain technology covering payments is not clear. If blockchain was an option in the early- to mid-1980s, when electronic payments were initially becoming a reality, the industry might have considered blockchain as the preferred technology platform to take us forward. However, I see no justification to rush the replacement of established and proven existing platforms with blockchain.

The distributed ledger concept creates interest to support 100 per cent service availability. It may simplify the situation when a network (with a traditional architecture) fails and transactions are not completed. The settlement process could also be simplified and the introduction of smart contracts may deliver benefits.

A key barrier to changing payment systems is the enormity of the task because the payment process infiltrates so many aspects of our daily existence. The gains must be substantial to justify the up-front investment and a period of upheaval.

Two payment applications for blockchain should be considered:

- RTGS (Real-Time Gross Settlement)
- RTP (Real-Time Payments)

RTGS systems generally operate in the domain of the Central Bank. It is a closed environment with limited external connections. Like a cryptocurrency system, all participants' accounts/funds reside in the RTGS/Central Bank domain. With lower transaction volumes than retail banking channels, such as EFTPOS and ATMS, a RTGS utilizing Blockchain should be feasible, providing the required security level is supported.

It should be mentioned that RTGS systems are not simple payment hubs, and managing financial institution liquidity is key when batch payment clearing often occurs overnight. Financial institutions' ability to clear payments can be challenged because of fluctuations in the liquidity position. This is a reason to support multiple settlement windows during the day to spread the settlement process through a 24-hour circle. Similarly, a benefit of introducing RTP services is to shift payments from end-of-day batch processing to near real-time throughout the day.

RTP systems TPS rates should exceed the blockchain limits. The actual person/ business-to-person/business payments would need to be off-chain with the settlement process between the financial institutions being on-chain. The deployment of RTP across all countries developed or otherwise is still in the early phase. A blockchain (off and on) RTP solution has a window available for new or first-time deployments.

Migration of RTGS systems to blockchain could be achieved through the circular process of system upgrading, impacting only the financial institutions and not their end customers.

China Union Pay

An association of bank members was established with the approval of the central bank, the People's Bank of China. Sound familiar! Supporting an interbank network, ATMs & EFTPOS for debit and credit cards that has become the largest international network based on transaction volume. Over 5 billion cards carry the logo. China Union Pay (CUP) cards are accepted in 168 countries and regions, and cards are issued in 48 countries. The actual transaction volume is not easily discoverable but the value for 2017 is reported to be US$14.980 trillion. That tells me the volume per card is US$2998 for 2017. It is not feasible to compare this figure with other countries. In Australia, on average, a person would hold 2.5 cards and spend on average more than AU$25,000 in 2017.

CUP has established an international subsidiary, UPI. The objective of this subsidiary is to grow CUP's international footprint. The effort has largely gone into the acceptance side of the business, enabling Chinese cardholders to use their card for payments overseas. CUP and UPI are providing their cardholders with a trusted payment option when they are travelling internationally.

In the early 1990s I spent some time (sponsored by Unisys) presenting, on multiple occasions, to the People's Bank of China on how electronic payment networks were architected. The bank was searching for knowledge and understanding across a range of payment methods. A colleague presented on the more traditional batch payment methods, which at that time the presentation was made were not quite so traditional. I am not claiming any rights to the success of the people's Bank of China, as I am sure it learnt far more from others and from its own experiences. What is interesting is to see the progress.

More recently UPI approached one of my clients to determine if they could partner with them in responding to a Middle East RFP. The RFP involved the delivery of a national electronic funds transfer system. My client was already committed to responding, and having UPI in the consortium would have delivered a compelling proposition. Unfortunately, the internal process for UPI to gain approval exceeded the time to respond and we needed to partner with an alternative provider.

I mention this to illustrate that in lower-tiered or less-developed countries there are opportunities for CUP and UPI to become a force. In particular, for them to build a stronger international issuing presence than they have today. CUP acquiring can be expected to follow the Chinese international traveller.

Bibliography

Capgemini, BNP Paribas (2017) *World Payments Report 2017*. www.worldpaymentsreport.com

Edgar Dunn & Company (June 2017) 11th Advanced Payments Report 2017. https://edgardunn.com/2017/06/2017-Advanced-Payments-report/

European Central Bank (2015) *Fourth Report on Card Fraud*. www.ecb.europa.eu/pub/pdf/other/4th_card_fraud_report.en.pdf

Financial Fraud Action (2016) *Fraud the Facts 2016*. www.financialfraudaction.org.uk/fraudfacts16/

Gervais, Arthur and Rami Khalil (2017) 'Revive: Rebalancing Off-Blockchain Payment Networks'. https://eprint.org/2017/823.pdf

Keenan, Tyler (8 November 2017) 'What is Ethereum?'. www.business2community.com/author/tyler-keenan

Loftus, Emma, head of global payments and FX (18 October 2017) Banking Technology ~ banking tech.com, JP Morgan Treasury Services.

Nakamoto, Satoshi, the founder(s) of Bitcoin (n.d.) 'Bitcoin: A Peer-to-Peer Electronic Cash System'. https://bitcoin.org/bitcoin.pdf

UK Cards Association (2017) *Fact and Figures*. www.theukcardsassociation.org.uk/facts_figures/index.asp

4

IMPACT OF MOBILE TECHNOLOGY

The mobile handset

The mobile phone handset has taken over almost all our lives as it has become a critical piece of technology. For many of us, it is no longer a phone but a device we all (without choice) use to be connected to the world. If we reject the mobile handset it could be argued that we no longer participate to any significant degree in society.

It would be interesting to know the amount of data that originates from or terminates at a mobile handset, where it originates from, and how it is delivered. And then to separate the data (or messages) into degrees of trivia and degrees of significance.

The terrestrial and mobile networks to the mobile handset user have become a seamless service, whether the service is delivered as mobile data or via Wi-Fi through a landline network. At the technology level, what has become the game changer is the 'Internet of Things' or the pervasiveness of IP (Internet Protocol).

We are all using the mobile handset less and less for what it was originally developed to deliver: the ability to make calls, communicate person to person. The change probably resulted when it was discovered a mobile handset could transfer text messages person to person. Then the smartphone arrived. I first became hooked on a Palm. Probably the best handset I have ever owned, only because at the time it provided a window on the future.

I rarely make a call on my mobile. Most of my messaging traffic is via email and many calls are through Skype, Zoom, WhatsApp, WebEx, etc. I have numerous apps to book hotels, access my bank accounts, transfer money, payment via the wallet, present airplane boarding passes, order and track a taxi, and the list goes on. I am not a social media person (outside of LinkedIn) but if I were, the portion of mobile calls and text messages in relation to other traffic would be even less.

My mobile is becoming more integral to my life. Take my phone away and I lose my identity. This has serious consequences and we are all exposed to some degree. If it has not yet, it will become a serious issue for the payments and banking industry. Regulators need to be actively involved in having security measures in place to ensure fraudsters, hacking into mobile handsets, cannot steal phone subscribers' identities.

The regulators need to work with the mobile manufacturers and their operating system providers to build a bulletproof device. That is, bulletproof for the critical data elements, especially those relating to the subscribers' identities and applications that provide access to services, specifically relating to banking and payments.

The payment industry in particular, as we have seen, does not really act until it is too late. And then we are in catch up mode, looking for technical solutions to plug the holes that fraudsters are walking through. The industry needs to become more proactive, anticipate the fraudsters' behaviour, and act in advance.

What are mobile payments?

There are many references to mobile payments. This term means something different depending on the specifics of the conversation.

I use my mobile handset to support the delivery of the following services:

- NFC payments.
- Mobile Banking payments, P2P and P2B.
- POS acceptance with a plug-in card reader and PIN pad.
- App to support discounted fuel purchases (pump activation) and payment.

All these services are covered by payments, but they are all different. So when the two words (mobile payments) are spoken or written I need the context. In all of the above services the mobile device can be substituted by another device. A mobile is just a user-interface option.

For NFC, a mobile phone is just a replacement of the form factor, the traditional payment card. Wearables also support NFC.

For mobile payments it is just an alternative to using a PC. Banks are developing mobile-specific apps, but good design supports a user switching from PC to mobile handset and back with little need for adjustment. The switch should be intuitive.

For POS, an app supports the user (merchant) interface and the device's connectivity to the network. This makes it a cheap option for a small or mobile merchant. The attached device enables the card to be inserted into the chip reader, supporting the EMV elements and the cardholder securely enters their PIN. If the cardholder requires a receipt, the app allows their email address to be entered. The merchant receives an email detailing each payment.

For the fuel app, again it is supporting a user interface also available with self-service pumps. The user enters the pump number and amount of fuel in dollars. If 'fill' is selected a default maximum value is requested. If the payment is preapproved the fuel is dispensed. This process is identical to using the self-service POS service at the pump, except that my payment card details are held on file along with my loyalty number.

You might argue I am being a little flippant and you are possibly correct, but apart from NFC I find all these services extremely useful. With some maturity NFC may join them. The critical point is that the mobile handset is the entry point into payment services that have existed for decades. The rails, as many refer to the networks, have not been replaced by the mobile handset.

I prefer to label mobile payment services utilizing text messages or the USSD (Unstructured Supplementary Service Data) channel as mobile money services. The handset-generated messages are exclusively transmitted by a handset and travel down the mobile communications channel. These services have been built and delivered specifically for the emerging economies and generally do not support interoperability. Emerging markets will be further discussed later in this chapter.

Mobile-to-mobile payments – UK

A mobile-to-mobile payment service was launched in April 2014. It is supported by 17 UK banks and building societies. The Australia NPP system was launched in February 2018 and supports an overlay to deliver a similar service.

The users of the service must register through their bank's banking app, providing their mobile number and the account to which it is linked. Users send money by logging onto their bank's mobile banking or payment app and enter the amount to be sent and the recipient's mobile number (which may be preloaded on a list).

Recipients to receive funds must be registered. If funds are sent to an unregistered mobile number the system sends a text instructing the recipient to register so their funds can be transferred into their nominated account.

The service is being used predominantly by subscribers under 45 years of age. It would be interesting to understand the reasons for this, other than the older age groups are perhaps less likely to use mobile technologies. If there was a user need, then age should not be a barrier to adoption with mobile penetration being so widespread. The average transaction value for the year ending 30 June 2017 was just under £50. For the same period 3.47 million transactions were sent.

This is a service needing to be watched. Daily usage is being restricted to £250. Perhaps the value limitations are restricting a broader age group adoption; although I doubt it.

Emerging markets – financial inclusion

An important focus for the payment industry over the last two decades has been the emerging markets. The payments industry has quickly gained momentum in these markets based on the belief that payments can be used to leverage economic development. The level of activity, especially relating to mobile money, has been intense.

The industry has been caught out with a shortage of skilled and experienced prac-
titioners plus a true understanding of the actual need or how to deliver a solution
that satisfies those needs – Kenya is the exception. With domestic banks in emerging markets being reluctant to commit, it has been left to mobile operators with the
support of the donor organizations and World Bank to deliver mobile money.
However, the services globally have only delivered a minimal success story, although
the momentum may be building in terms of acceptance levels.

A core challenge has been the ability to deliver a cost effective service to markets
that lack the basic infrastructural requirements, such as electricity and mobile
coverage. As with all payment services, the challenge is to develop services the end
users will adopt because the services meet the end users' needs. What may be seen
by the donor organizations as a perfect solution most likely ignores many of the
nuances of an emerging economy.

However, on the positive side, rationalization is underway and effective solutions are evolving for these markets.

The mobile operators embraced mobile money as an opportunity for reducing
churn and driving up the average revenue per unit (ARPU), and mobile money
provides the opportunity to deliver additional revenue into low revenue-generating
markets. The business model for mobile operators is simply based on delivering
added value (fee-based) services.

Although mobile technology addresses the communication challenge, not
understanding all the challenges, plus ignoring the basic principles of payment
system development learnt by the developed markets, has resulted in significant
waste.

The *GSMA Report 2017: State of the Industry Report on Mobile Money*, claims that
the top performers have 'cracked the recipe' for success. They have apparently
achieved this by serving a wider ecosystem through integrating with seven or more
banks or, on average:

- 95 billers,
- 31 organizations for bulk disbursements,
- 6500 merchants.

This has increased their average revenue per active customer from the overall
average of US$1.2 to $1.7. The *GSMA Report 2017: State of the Industry Report on
Mobile Money*, reported that revenue was US$2.4 billion, providing a year-on-year
increase of 34 per cent.

What this indicates is that for a mobile money service to be successful it must
open up to a greater range of market participants, rather than operating in a closed
environment. What is not mentioned here is interoperability between mobile
money providers in the same eco-system. This will be necessary to increase the
merchant base to greater levels. The Global System for Mobile Communications
Association (GSMA) indicates 6500 merchants or 128 active accounts per merchant, which is a reasonable level, especially if agents are excluded. In comparison,

Australia has 48 accounts per POS device or 26 individuals per POS device. Not exactly comparable but if the mobile money providers could lower the 128 closer to the Australian POS number transaction then volumes would rise without doubt.

A 2014 study by the GSMA identified scale as critical. Scale in a payment system is measured by transaction volume. Volume drives down cost, delivering the potential for lower fees, which will stimulate growth. Further broadening the levels of acceptance enhances the user proposition. You might say this increases the usefulness of the service.

A significant factor in achieving scale for the cards market was when a merchant signed up to accept cards issued from one bank (acquirer) who was a member of an eco-system enabling the merchant to accept all cards with the same brand. In the early years, these eco-systems were domestic, within a country or region.

It would be of value to all mobile money providers within a single market to be supported by this same approach through interoperability. In effect, to create one large market place rather than segmentation, with individual merchants being owned by a singular mobile operator. I find this lack of cooperation in the mobile money space intriguing. Generally, mobile networks provide an interoperable service where one subscriber can call or text subscribers contracted to a competitive network. Doing this increased the size of the user base (market) and allowed all participants to compete on the basis of service level and price.

There was an attempt to implement such a service in Nepal but it was struggling because the market participants were unable to see the benefits of a collective approach and not prepared to participate.

Mobile money market penetration levels

The most significant indicator of penetration levels is the percentage of active accounts. The *GSMA Report 2017, State of the Industry Report on Mobile Money* informs us that the global percentage is 34 per cent. So for every 100 mobile subscribers who signed up to the mobile money service only 34 are users. This percentage may be distorted by inactive accounts not being closed when the balance is near zero and no activity has occurred for an extended period. This is often the case with card accounts where there is a reluctance to close inactive accounts as it makes the statistics less impressive.

The average active accounts for East Asia & Pacific are surprisingly low considering this region includes the Philippines and Indonesia. The Philippines, along with Kenya, was a pioneering mobile money country with both Smart Communications and Globe entering the Philippine payments market in the early 2000s. This same region has had comparatively low growth over the 12 month period of 2016/2017, which may be an indication that for mobile money it has reached maturity.

The Sub-Saharan African region, which includes Kenya, is leading based on the number of active accounts, with South Asia well behind in second place. However, based on the percentage of active accounts, the Latin America and Caribbean region is well ahead of the other regions, with 50+ per cent. This is still lower than the optimum or desirable, which should be near 80 per cent if not higher.

Mobile money transaction levels

The GSMA report also covers the number of transactions generated, on average, from the active accounts. The transaction level will be driven by services. If the service is just a remittance channel it will deliver only a few transactions per month per active account. Of the regions covered in the report, only Sub-Saharan Africa has transaction levels suggesting more activity than remittances and/or P2P transactions.

What is also of interesting is the average transaction value. East Asia and the Pacific, with an average value for 2017 of US$64.41, greatly exceed the next placed region, Sub-Saharan Africa which has an average value of only US$16.58 for 2017. The higher transaction value for East Asia and the Pacific suggests the average remittance from overseas workers is higher, possibly resulting from the economic status of the source countries.

Again, referring to the *GSMA Report 2017: State of the Industry Report Mobile Money*, the transaction spread given in Table 4.1 has been compiled. The percentages are based on value (not volume), accumulated inward, outward and within network.

Not surprising in this table is the low percentage of remittances. Cash in and out plus P2P accounts for 80 per cent of the transactions in 2017, down from 89 per cent in 2012. With these types of statistics one can always expect a margin of error, in my experience. A 2 per cent increase for Merchant and bill payments is disappointing over a 5-year period.

This raises the issue of the suitability of mobile money for transactions outside of being a cash transition service. By this I mean a service for transferring funds electronically where the receiver does not withdraw all in cash from an agent but uses the service to initiate electronically payments to other parties. MPesa in Kenya is a service that has moved in this direction.

TABLE 4.1 Transaction spread

Transaction classification	Percentage	
	2012	*2017*
Cash	60	55
Bank to wallet to bank	2	5
Merchant/bill payments	5	9
Remittances	4	6
P2P	29	25
Total	100	100

Source: Data from *GSMA Report 2017: State of the Industry Report on Mobile Money*.

TABLE 4.2 Mobile money movement

Category	2012	2017
Inward (%)	36	40
Circulating (%)	30	27
Outgoing (%)	34	33

Source: Data from *GSMA Report 2017: State of the Industry Report on Mobile Money.*

Again, looking at the GSMA report we can look at the percentage split between the three categories, see Table 4.2.

The value of the mobile money services globally has increased five times over the 5 years. The percentage of the funds circulating or exiting the service in 2017 over 2012 has dropped, indicating funds are being held within the service. In 2017, inward over outgoing was US$2.2 billion compared with US$0.1 billion in 2012. The challenge for the service providers is that, as more funds are held within Mobile Money services, the individual owners of those funds will look for interest to be accrued (earned). This suggests mobile money users are moving towards the need for a banking service.

Achieving more from mobile money

The challenge is to move mobile money from a cash transfer service to a payment service. The impression given by many mobile money champions is that their underlying goal is to drive banks out of business. The rational approach is to build a mobile banking/payment service meeting the needs of the unbanked or under-banked and, in doing so, develop a partnership with the banks to deliver a far more inclusive service. The top mobile money service providers based on the *GSMA Report 2017* have recognized that integration with main street banking is a critical success factor.

The banks' business model has been built to service (perhaps not consciously) those with higher income and more complex service needs than the under-banked and unbanked. Banks are simply unable to service those at the bottom of the socio-economic pyramid effectively, not only in terms of cost but also in terms of delivery. Individuals from this sector are not comfortable in visiting a bank branch or are not familiar with technology-based delivery services such as ATMs.

An issue with this sector is also the identification of unbanked individuals. Regulators require banks to enforce KYC (know your customer) processes. Countries such as India and the Philippines have initiated projects to introduce citizen identification based on biometrics. This enables KYC for the opening of bank accounts.

The India Reserve Bank in 2006 took the initiative to introduce regulations to support the concept of Correspondent Banks (CB). CBs deliver 'no frills' accounts through an agency network by being aligned to one or more of the state banks. A selective group of private banks also joined the initiative. CBs were originally established by NGOs and non-profit organizations but now the commercial sector has become involved.

The CB services cover:

- Cash deposits
- Withdrawals
- Remittances
- Balance enquiries
- Small value credit facilities
- Insurances

A study I undertook for IFC in 2011, across India and Nepal, identified that each CB was developing its own solution. There was not a common approach and therefore no standardization. The only common factor was that mobile played a role in supporting the agents within each network.

The issue with this approach was there being no interoperability between the CB. A CB could not accept payment instructions from a customer of another CB.

This was not necessarily a short-term problem but with the maturing of the services it could be a limiting factor. The Indian Reserve Bank (IRB) was possibly singularly focused on the delivery of a service, quickly with the view that limitations could be addressed in the future. A benefit of this approach was an insight into the most appropriate services for the market segment being targeted.

It is understood that, more recently, the IRB has addressed the interoperability issue. As interoperability supports interchange it is a critical factor for developing a national payment system.

High profile successes

A few high profile successes are always quoted, such as Smart Money in the Philippines and MPesa in Kenya.

Smart Money

A solution I was involved with at the architectural and system integration level was Smart Communications' Smart Money solution in the Philippines. The initial development was undertaken in 2000–2002.

This solution was quite sophisticated as the mobile handset was linked to a debit card (MasterCard) and an account that supported real-time updates. The system also linked to retail banks so funds could be moved between the two domains.

A SIM Toolkit application with security elements was developed to support a range of basic transactions, (similar to what would be supported by an ATM as well as P2P payments) from the handset. The security level that was developed supported handset PIN entry. A common PIN was used for both card and mobile money.

The MasterCard plastic card could be used like any other card and was therefore accepted at POS (retailers) and ATMs domestically and internationally.

The Smart Communications agency network became the Smart Money network. Smart also established overseas remittance agencies in places such as Singapore, where there is a significant population of Filipino workers to enable funds to be sent home to their families.

You could argue this is not solely a solution for the unbanked, but also for the underbanked and the banked.

Smart Communications also developed the Smart Money infrastructure as an airtime reseller service. This supported a wide network of resellers enabling many Filipinos to earn an income, delivering social benefits.

Smart Money was ahead of its time and I therefore do not believe many understood the capability and deployment scope of this solution.

MPesa

MPesa was developed by Safaricom – a mobile operator in Kenya that was 40 per cent owned by Vodafone – and came four to five years after Smart Money and was based on SMS messaging. MPesa did not have the domain crossover of Smart Money and was narrower in scope.

It could be claimed that MPesa was more successful than Smart Money because it was designed to satisfy a far more straightforward need, in a market that was far less complex. The Philippines has both domestic and international remittance streams, with established competitors.

Prior to MPesa, remittances in cash had to be delivered to recipients in rural villages by bus or truck. There was a reliance on the honesty of the drivers and a non-regulated fee would be charged. A safer and more secure delivery channel needed to be developed.

The solution was a mobile service based on an agency network.

The challenge for these types of networks is to ensure agents have the cash. In Kenya, recipients of funds began not to take the full amount so the remittance service provider became a deposit taker. To help the situation, agents were also store holders/suppliers of produce enabling the funds to be used to make purchases directly from the agent. MPesa delivered an excellent business opportunity for agents.

MPesa supported:

*   Withdrawal of cash.
*   Storage of money (deposits).
*   Payments.
*   Remittances.
*   Airtime purchases.

The point is that from a simple money transfer solution a remittance system developed into no frills banking services. There have been attempts to replicate

MPesa by other mobile operators in other countries. However, it has been reported that they have not achieved the same level of success. MPesa obviously satisfied a need at the time and was implemented with the support of the regulator in a manner that was appropriate for the Kenyan eco-system.

Maldives

In 2005 I was requested by CGAP (Consultative Group to Assist the Poor) to assist in a project to determine whether a mobile payment service should be deployed in the Maldives. I would not classify the Maldives as an emerging market although its national economic statistics might suggest otherwise. Maldives has two corner-stones to its economy: tourism and fisheries. It had a high penetration of mobile phones.

It was the fishing industry that was the focus. The Maldives consists of near 1200 islands over 90,000 square kilometres, occupied by only 0.3+ million inhabitants. So it is a unique situation of a small population spread across a large geographical area, which mostly consists of water. Services, public and commercial, are centred on the capital, Male.

The challenge was cash management. Cash needed to be couriered out to the islands so fishermen could be paid. The fishermen then took time off from fishing (2–3 days), normally monthly, to go to Male (where the cash had come from) to buy supplies, pay bills and bank their surplus cash. This was totally inefficient and costly for all involved.

The business case easily stacked up. The project to develop a mobile solution was completed but the solution was not implemented for unexplained reasons. I suspect the underlying cause of the failure was project creep and a conflict of interest between the various affected parties. I was not involved in the RFP (Request for Proposal) preparation process because of a conflict of interest as I was a shareholder in a company with ambitions of bidding and winning the business. I did receive a copy of the RFP document. The scope had expanded beyond the requirements, in my view, of what a country of 300,000 people needed. I do suspect it might have been the case of 'while we have the chance let's do everything'.

I was quite excited by the original scope and thought the Maldives were in a unique position to demonstrate how a mobile service could replace cash and improve the lives of the inhabitants. Today, one would implement a RTP system with the user interfaces being based on the PTM platform. The Maldives simply needed a system that would support money transfer and bill payment.

Pacific Islands

In more recent years I was involved in delivering a feasibility study to connect a mobile payment solution to the Visa network by linking mobile accounts to a Visa Card. This was similar, in principle, to elements of Smart Money, connecting a mobile money system and the banking system.

The mobile payment service was underperforming and a core reason was that remittances transferred into the mobile accounts could not be accessed conveniently by the recipients. The agency network was not reaching out to the community of recipients. The ability to use ATMs and present a card at merchants (EFTPOS) for payment or for cash-out may have gone some way to addressing the problem, but was unlikely to fully meet the need.

For mobile money to be successful I believe there is a need for a certain density in population. An observation was made by a commentator some years ago that population density was a key success factor for Kenya's MPesa. The Indian CB program has been targeted at areas/cities of a certain population.

The feasibility study produced a negative outcome. The mobile payment solution was not compliant with any international standard and enhancing the software to support interoperability was not feasible.

Alipay

Alipay is best described as a mobile money (and payments) solution. It has approximately 520 million users with a presence in 110 countries. Its international presence is focused on acceptance. A question I am now regularly asked by Chinese business colleagues and clients is: will Alipay be adopted internationally?

There are two elements of Alipay that need to be understood prior to answering this question:

- Electronic wallet (or purse)
- The QR Code user interface

The electronic wallet, or should we refer to it as a purse, is far from unique. Many systems particular in the world of mobile money are based on a purse, as are mass transit systems. Purses are core to supporting financial inclusion for the under-banked or unbanked communities as well as for prepaid services.

There are common aspects between Alipay and PayPal. Both support e-commerce, both from a wallet, which allows customers to maintain funds in a purse. Alipay has broader payment scope with its retail acceptance using QR codes.

The user interface is mobile based. QR codes is an approach used to avoid the issuing of cards or supporting NFC for card-present payments. The QR code is scanned rather than a card being presented. User participation centres on the mobile phone.

It can be argued that as Alipay is based on QR codes there is a lot more scope or versatility associated with the payment service. Greater levels of data can be captured. This is further enhanced as the system is not supporting a global community of card issuers and acquirers.

See https://docs.alipay.com/global/publicapi/ztkgl5 for more details on Alipay.

International Alipay adoption

It would be rare to see a purse replace a bank account in the banked or overbanked communities. In fact, the way an Alipay wallet would be implemented is by integrating the service with banks directly through an API (Application Programming Interface) and/or a real-time payment service, with transfers being initiated by the wallet holder. Similarly, funds could be transferred back to the user's bank account via the same channels. Card-initiated reload would also be feasible but potentially more costly.

One could ask, with APIs, why have a wallet? Alipay could directly access the user's funds in their bank account for each transaction, similar to the way a debit card works today, and assuming the appropriate authorization and authentication is in place.

Two factors will drive Alipay in the developed payments market:

- Chinese tourists visiting the various countries will expose the brand to the international market.
- Alibaba e-commerce business has the potential to provide a need for the western consumer to sign up to Alipay. We return to payments as an enabler of commerce. There needs to be a strong commercial reason for a new payment method to be adopted, and the purchasing of Chinese products online by non-Chinese citizens could be the reason.

From a payment prospect, Alipay is not a threat to the banking sector as such but to the card schemes and PSPs. Banks that are also card acquirers would find their volume impacted but in many countries banks have reduced their involvement in the card acquiring channels. Alipay would be a new payment channel, built on its own set of rails. Alipay therefore is a real threat to Visa and MasterCard.

The only potential hurdle to international expansion could be regulations, but I assume Alipay is able to satisfy this requirement. The other major concern is how Alipay would stand up to the fraudster community. No doubt the fraudsters would look to exploit any weaknesses in the Alipay channel.

A final comment: it is easier to fill a void than it is to replace an incumbent service.

Change of approach

I look at these mobile developments and wonder, if starting over, would the same path be followed. We are currently in the space where the capability because of smartphones is taking a huge leap forward, but smartphone penetration rates are still low in critical countries.

Ericsson has projections out to 2023 based on regions, comparing the number of smartphones in circulation with feature phones that will still be in use (see www.ericsson.com/TET/trafficView/loadBasicEditor.ericsson).

Ericson has estimated the global 2018 smartphone market (subscriptions) penetration over feature phones is 63 per cent. The 2023 estimate for smartphones is 81 per cent.

The situation in the South East Asia/Oceania region is that smartphones are currently setting at 57 per cent market share. Ericsson forecast this percentage in 2023 to reach 84 per cent. Smartphones in the Middle East and Africa are currently at 48 per cent, increasing to 81 per cent, and India is currently at 42 per cent and expected in 2023 to reach 71 per cent.

When considering mobile payments for emerging markets it would seem that feature phones are going to be with us for a considerable period. We can assume 19 per cent of subscribers will still be using feature phones in 2023 and, in the regions requiring mobile payment services, the percentage will be higher. This limits our scope to be creative.

If given the opportunity to revisit a Maldives type situation I would consider recommending a Smartphone RTP based solution. The smartphone penetration is reported to be high, and internet usage is high so the technology barriers are not present. The country does not have a high population so introducing change should be feasible. Simply replacing or swapping out all existing feature phones with smartphones would not be a major challenge. Payment instruments such as cheques could be quickly phased out. There should be no need for an ACH (Automatic Clearing House) as all payments could be moved to real-time clearing and settlement. An Australian NPP settlement approach would remove the need for a full function RTGS system.

The Maldives' banks, if they haven't already, should deploy a mobile banking service supporting both intra-bank and inter-bank money transfers, bill payments as well as international money transfers, plus the standard customer account enquires, and so on.

Bibliography

Ericsson (June 2018) *Ericsson Mobility*. www.ericsson.com/TET/trafficView/loadBasicEditor. ericsson

GSMA (n.d.) *GSMA Report 2017: State of the Industry Report on Mobile Money*. www.gsma. com/mobilefordevelopment/sotir/

5

PAYMENT SERVICES AND METHODS

Where electronic payments started – ATMs

For the first eight or so years of my payments career, ATMs played a significant part. ATMs were the first mass market electronic delivery channel and many of today's practices come from the learning gained through building and implementing ATM services. You could almost say the ATM was the Ford Model T of the electronic payments industry.

I actually saw my first ATM in 1974 in Oxford Street in London. The device read the card and kept it, dispensing a pre-set amount. I assumed it was to cater for the Englishman's need for cash after being expelled from a pub at closing time, having spent all his cash and having the need to purchase a fare home. This was the period prior to the Indian curry becoming the after-pub indulgence. By the time I became involved, the card-eating ATM machines had been replaced.

The motivation for banks to introduce ATMs was to shift customers out of in-branch teller queues. The business case was based on shifting customers who only wanted cash to ATMs where they could be served quicker and more cheaply. ATMs were installed in walls at high foot traffic branches.

Did this work? The service was a success in terms of customer acceptance but it did not deliver the anticipated cost savings. The frequency of use meant total ATM transaction cost in the markets I worked in equated to the total cost of the less frequent but more expensive branch transactions. Regardless, ATMs were at the forefront of bank customers taking up an electronic delivery service that would lead to the reshaping of banking into what we have today. Often there would be no teller queues in a branch and a long queue for the ATMs outside. It became clear bank customers did not really like going into a branch. Wonder why!

Initially, ATMs gave banks a competitive advantage. As acceptance grew, ATMs became a 'must provide' service. ATMS in effect became a commodity. They no longer delivered a point of difference. Banks willingly joined shared networks not only to generate revenue but also to manage cost. Bank customers' 'trust' in the service was established along with their need for convenience. Customers became comfortable using another bank's device assuming cost was minimal.

Banks would originally manage and service their own networks, but with the competitive edge disappearing and the cost of devices falling, banks moved to outsourcing. The ISO model gained traction, especially in the lower volume locations. Banks focused on ATMs in their branches and in high-volume main street locations. ATMs became a point of presence for the owning bank's brand.

The type of ATMs that initially dominated the market was the IBM3624, an expensive device. These devices required support from an ATM hosting platform, an expensive telecommunications loop protocol, plus they needed to be monitored and serviced. Initially, ATMs were only available during banking hours but very quickly their hours were extending to 24, 365/6 days a year. This brought security issues and the need for surveillance. Devices initially installed in the wall in branches went into non-bank sites. In-lobby machines went initially into branch lobbies but soon found their way into shopping malls, etc. Now we have cheap cash-dispensing devices in convenience stores, serviced by the retailer and running off EFTPOS networks rather than the established ATM networks.

Costings

In general terms, costings back in the early days for a cash withdrawal over the branch counter were estimated at approximately US$2.50 (depending on market). The cost of an ATM cash withdrawal was US$0.50, delivering a ratio of five ATM transactions for every branch transaction. This sounds like a strong business case for ATMs. In practice, it was not a 1-to-1 substitution. Bank customers were visiting ATMs almost daily, whereas they only visited branches once a week, or even less frequently. Many bank customers were using ATMS to just take out the cash they needed for the current day or the weekend. They were a budgeting tool for managing their finances.

For an ATM to break-even in the early years, a through-the-wall machine would need to generate 6500 transactions per month, whereas an in-lobby machine break-even was about 3500 transactions. The average monthly transactions per ATM in the early years was near to 12,000. It would be rare for a machine to achieve 22,000 plus transactions each month. Although machines in locations with 24-hour high foot traffic could be expected to achieve higher transaction levels.

These numbers would have varied from market to market but they provide a benchmark. Today's equivalent numbers would be half those, with the numbers for cash dispensers found in convenience stores being even lower.

Most banks saw their ATM network as a cost centre and attempted to recover costs through interchange fees. One of the banks I worked with in the late 1980s took the opposing view that their ATM network was a profit centre. This bank had a small card base and, although their ATM network was also small, their ratio of cards to ATMs was low. Therefore, they had surplus ATM capacity available to the cardholders of their interchange partners, enabling net positive interchange revenue to be earnt.

To maximize their profit, this bank focused on service reliability and the astute positioning of its devices in high foot traffic locations. Location, location, location was the catchphrase for all ATM network managers chasing interchange revenue. This is why busy city intersections have ATMs on all corners. Even if not chasing the interchange revenue, a bank should be out to minimize the interchange they pay.

This was all 25 plus years ago and is probably still relevant in less-developed payment markets. In the very developed markets, ATMs have become a mature channel with a potentially limited future as cash usage declines and the proliferation of low cost devices being installed by ISO-type organizations compete for volume. As a generalization, ISOs charge higher fees. In many cases banks will not charge their own customers but will charge other bank customers.

A trend is to replace (encouraged or enforced by regulators) interchange fees with a direct fee to the cardholder. Regulators require the fee to be displayed and accepted before the transaction is initiated. Regulators are responding to pressure from consumer groups for fees and charges to be transparent.

Extending the life of the delivery channel

In a number of markets the personal banking machine (PBM) was introduced. This was a device supporting an extended set of transactions such as the depositing cheques and paying bills. A number of banks created secure self-service lobbies accessed by a payment card, housing a number of PBM devices.

This type of facility was not universally adopted as many banks focused primarily on cash out, balance enquiries and the ability for customers to transfer funds between their own accounts. Banks did not want customers requiring only cash to be held up in queues with customers paying their bills and reconciling their bank balances. In this case, if banks wanted to provide these extended services, then they installed within their lobbies non-cash devices alongside cash-only devices.

In other markets, such as Russia, the ATM has developed into a self-service kiosk with a capability of delivering non-banking related services such as purchasing event tickets.

Like all payment services, economies are only achieved through scale measured in transaction volume. Volume reduces the cost per transaction so the introduction of new devices with extended or new capabilities needs to be supported by higher transaction volume. In many markets this volume could not be achieved by PBMs and therefore they were not installed or were quickly phased out.

In some markets we have now Smart ATMs. What is a Smart ATM? The Westpac New Zealand website (www.westpac.co.nz/assets/Personal/Your-Money-and-Tailored-Packs/Brochures/ways_to_bank.pdf) provides the answer.

Our Smart ATMs are all about offering a quick and easy self-service option that allows you to do your banking when it's convenient for you. Benefits of our Smart ATMs include:

- Ability to bank outside of normal hours (many Smart ATMs are available 24/7).
- Cash/coin deposits that are immediately credited to your account.
- Cheque deposits, with a receipt that includes an image of the cheque for your records.
- Ability to make deposits into other Westpac accounts.
- Deposits treated as electronic transactions, helping many account types avoid manual 'over the counter' transaction fees.

These Smart ATMs are similar to the PBMs. This is the industry trying to drag the last few transactions out of this declining payment channel by going back to the future. The newer devices supported by open platform (PC) technologies are more suitable for delivering these services than the old devices.

To be able to deposit cash, including coins, as well as cheques may prove useful for small merchants. My cynical side suggests that taking an image of the cheque is an excellent service. It will allow bank customers to frame the cheque and hang it on their office wall with a little placard, 'The last cheque I ever received'.

The future

Is there a future for ATMs? As long as there is a need for cash there will be a need for ATMs. I made a statement in the late 1990s that ATMs had a limited life, with the demand for cash declining and with the option in many markets for 'cash-out' at the point of sale. I have been reminded of this statement by colleagues, as ATMs are still part of our lives.

In countries where the need for cash is reducing then ATM numbers cannot be expected to increase nor will older devices, I suspect, be replaced.

As volume declines, the cost per transaction logically should increase. The volume of ATM transactions may be declining but the cost of devices has also fallen. Changes in the technology must have brought down the cost of ownership, but there will be a break-even point where the transaction volume drops to an unsupportable level.

Banks are likely to retain an ATM presence, for branding purposes, in locations to service their own customers' demands. This may be where Smart ATMs are or will be located. Banks will need to map customer/usage behaviour to ensure the right device is installed for a location.

The data for Figure 5.1 are sourced from statistics published by the Reserve Bank of Australia, covering its eco-system. The Australian payment market is mature and the chart indicates that my prediction of the late 1990s was too optimistic by a decade, but a decline is now evident.

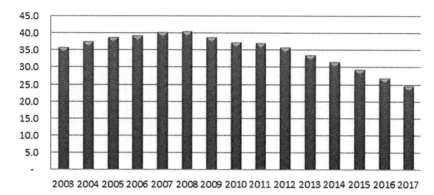

FIGURE 5.1 Cash withdrawals per inhabitant – Australia

Source: Data from the Reserve Bank of Australia Statistics C4.

Figure 5.1 clearly indicates a decline in the Australian use of ATMs over the last 9 to 10 years, with cash withdrawal transactions per inhabitant peaking in 2008 at almost 41 before dropping below 25 in 2017.

Figure 5.2 shows the British visit their ATMs more frequently in recent years than Australians but the drop off indicates a consistent trend (sourced from www. link.co.uk).

The question should be asked whether people are still withdrawing the same amount of cash. For Australians, for the month of January 2003, a cash withdrawal had an average value of AUD174.48 and for the month of June 2017 that value had risen to AUD221.02. That is a percentage increase of a little under 27 per cent.

Figure 5.3 shows the year on year growth in cash withdrawal value.

There is consistency between the graphs. The years 2007–2009 were the period that ATMs in Australia reached their peak. The decline between 2008 and 2017 in yearly withdrawal value has been 29 per cent.

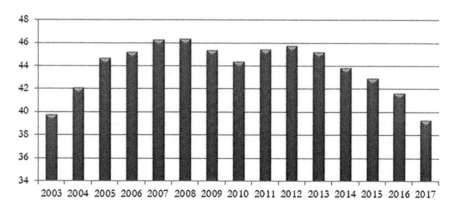

FIGURE 5.2 ATM cash withdrawal per inhabitant – UK

Source: Data from www.link.co.uk.

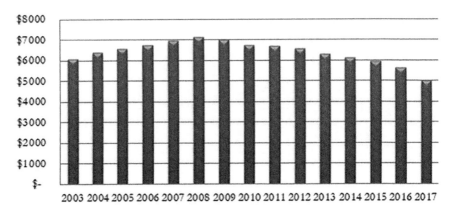

FIGURE 5.3 Yearly average cash withdrawal per inhabitant Australian

Source: Data from Reserve Bank of Australia Statistics C4.

For each country, the timing of this decline will be different and if the decline has not already started it will occur as the non-cash payment channels develop.

The dream of many is a cashless society. In a number of countries this is on the horizon and ATMs are obviously the channel that will be most affected.

It is important to note that during depressed economic periods, evidence suggests people revert to cash. Maybe cash in our pockets is considered easier to manage and enables us to restrain our spending whereas the electronic form is psychologically not considered as real. This is supported by Figure 5.3 with the GFC 2007/8.

ATM contradiction

I said earlier in the section on ATMs that the numbers of devices will reduce as usage declines. In Australia that is not yet happening and, in fact, ATM numbers have increased, based on RBA statistics, from 20,339 in 2003 to 32,191 in 2017.

Figure 5.4 shows the decrease in inhabitants per device.

This graph suggests the number of people per ATM is plateauing before perhaps climbing back. The highest saturation of devices in the market was reached in 2011 at 740.9 and it has fluctuated marginally over the last 6 years.

The United Kingdom chart, Figure 5.5, illustrates the same trend, although the number of people per device is 25 per cent higher than the Australian figure.

We can conclude that ATM usage is declining but ATM device numbers have not yet been impacted. Are ATM numbers insensitive to volume or is simply the cost of ATMs both, in terms of capital investment and operational expenditure, correspondingly reduced? Possibly it is just timing, with many installed ATMs not yet reaching the end of their lives. In the near future, a number of older devices may be decommissioned and not replaced, at which point the inhabitants per ATM will climb sharply.

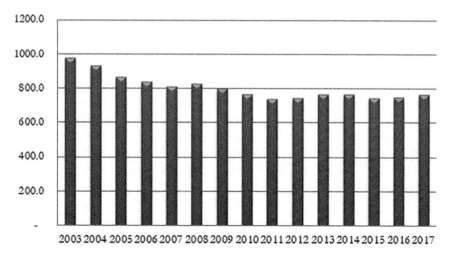

FIGURE 5.4 Inhabitants per ATM – Australia

Source: Data from Reserve Bank of Australia Statistics C4.

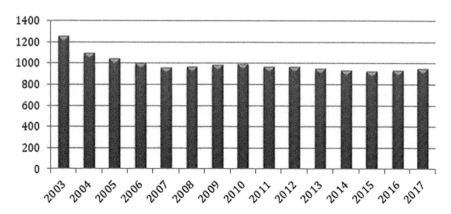

FIGURE 5.5 Inhabitants per ATM – UK

Source: Data from www.link.co.uk.

ATM interchange proposition

In the early 1990s, after I left Databank I had a contract with the New Zealand Trust Bank Group. This banking organization at the time was owned by regional community trusts. It had built up an impressive ATM network on a commitment to service its communities. Therefore, many devices had low monthly transaction volumes. The trust banks considered their ATM network to be a point of differ-ence when they were compared with the trading banks. There was no way they were ever going to open up their network to a competitor – until a new CEO arrived. This new CEO obviously looked at the operational cost of their ATM network and decided action was required. The result being that I was offered a contract to develop a business case for accepting other-bank issued ATM cards. The business case needed to be strong to counter the internal resistance. For not the first time in my career, I was to become an enemy of the traditionalist, an agent for change.

The assignment was interesting as I took the learnings from the smaller trading bank that treated their ATM network as a profit centre and applied those learnings to the larger Trust Bank Group. Without question, the Trust Bank's ATMs had a sizable profit potential that was not being realized. The ratio of cards on issue to ATMs installed was out of balance, resulting in a network with unused capacity. Consideration had to be given that any interchange agreement gives cardholders of all participating banks the option to use any ATM covered by the agreement. The net gain or loss needs to be considered. For banks with a very small card base the option to pay interchange fees may be considered more cost effective. The overriding benefit of interchange agreements is that cardholders of all parties have improved access to the service.

For Trust Bank, their ATMs with low transaction volumes helped build the business case, as many were located in small rural towns where their device was the only device. Although a majority of the population of these towns may have banked with the Trust Bank, not all did. There were the travellers through these towns to be considered.

The trading bank ATM network (the other significant network) was not based on a centralized switch so there was the requirement to connect bi-laterally to each bank. Negotiations had to be completed with each bank and we needed to prioritize the banks to plan the order of connecting.

A comprehensive model of the country's ATM usage was developed. We also determined each bank's card-to-ATM device ratio. As previously mentioned, we also needed to consider that Trust Bank customers would be able to use the trading banks ATMs.

The banks were prioritized on their highest number of customers per ATM as this was considered the factor that would drive positive net interchange revenue.

As a contractor, I moved on before the full benefits of opening up the Trust Bank network was realized. I was told it was extremely successfully.

As ATM usage declines, owners of ATM networks are going to need to work harder to make profits. Understanding usage patterns through modelling will be critical. Knowing who is using your ATMs and their bank will allow a strategy to be developed.

With non-cash transactions being delivered through internet services (mobile, tablet and PC), ATM network owners will need to become more innovative in terms of services or simply look to rationalize and reduce their service footprint. Rationalizing the network through interchange with competitors may prove the only survival approach. Banks may revert to ATMs only being positioned at their branches, although in some markets banks are closing branches. ATMs then become the only point of presence, a location for a SMART ATM perhaps.

ATMs falling usage – a trend to a cashless state

We need to be careful in jumping to this conclusion.

Transaction Network Services, in their September 2017 publication, *Global Variance in ATM Usage* forces us to look at this topic a little closer.

The report covered the UK, the USA and Australia. Those in these countries surveyed who do not use ATMs were, respectively, 10 per cent, 29 per cent and 16 per cent. On the opposing side, 35 per cent of Australians stated they did not need cash any longer compared with the USA at 29 per cent and the UK at 27 per cent.

A key factor was that although 29 per cent of USA citizens surveyed did not use ATMs, 37 per cent stated that they preferred to obtain their cash from bank branches, over the counter. Comparable figure for the UK was 29 per cent and for Australia it was down at 19 per cent. Those adults surveyed seemed to mistrust ATMs (loss of personal details) or felt they were at risk from criminal activity.

Whether these factors, particularly loss of personal details would inhibit the same adults using other electronic delivery channels was not covered. 'Do they use EFTPOS?' would be an interesting question to ask. Internet banking as it can be used in the privacy of one's home is possibly acceptable. Is age a significant factor? I would not think so as ATMs have been with us for three to four decades.

ATM legacy

ATMs introduced the ubiquitous plastic payment card to support self-service. Bank customers adopted the ATM card and quickly trusted the services. The cards linked the cardholder to their accounts and allowed the account holder to be authenticated electronically.

ATM networks represented the starting point and electronic payments have grown at a rapid rate.

Many of the initial messaging and security standards were developed for ATMs, to be adopted and further developed for EFTPOS. Interoperability supporting interchange and shared payment networks were also pioneered by ATM services. The ATM built bank customer trust in electronic banking services, breaking down any fear their money would not be safe.

Point of sale (EFTPOS or POS)

A key factor with the electronic funds transfer at the point of sale (EFTPOS) was its development as two separate systems, which still operate today. I was recently reminded of this when making a duty free purchasing at Sydney airport. I presented my Australian-issued Visa debit card and went to 'tap and go' but was stopped by the sales assistant. She informed me if I either used 'tap and go' or inserted my card and pressed credit she would need to add a 3 per cent surcharge. Alternatively, if I inserted my card and pressed current or savings there would be no charge.

In Australia, as is the case in other countries, there are two networks, a card scheme and the proprietary bank scheme. A single device accepts all card types and account selection determines the rails used in Australia. Other countries with a similar arrangement distinguish the two through the card type, either accepted by the same or different terminals.

It is also common to have multiple proprietary bank networks. Greater efficiency is gained from a national propriety bank network, with lower costs being delivered by a single system infrastructure.

So, in many countries, the POS devices accepting all cards (or nearly all) have become the standard, with interchange supported either by an in-country switching service or by the card schemes' networks. Devices also have the capability to route transactions to a specific network based on BIN/IIN. In other countries retailers have a number of POS devices. In the Philippines I counted 18 on a cashier's counter and I am sure other retailers had more. Retailers for each card presented choose the device provided by the acquirer offering the lowest merchant discount rate.

With a North American colleague, I built a business case to support one device accepting all cards at a competitive merchant discount fee. Although the business case would support a one for 18 swap-out, we could not gain any support from the Philippines card payment business sector.

History behind EFTPOS development

For countries with an established ATM network, EFTPOS was simply taking advantage of a high penetration of ATM cards and extending their acceptance into the retail sector. The same card could be used to obtain cash from an ATM and to pay for goods and services at the point of sale, where in both cases a PIN was used to authenticate the cardholder. These are the cards generically referred to as proprietary debit cards.

The electronic acceptance of credit cards was first achieved through EDC, electronic data capture at the point of sale. EDC was limited to capturing the transaction details and supporting the authorization process. EDC did not authenticate the cardholder, just the availability of funds and the card status. The docket printed by the device had to be signed by the cardholder. EDC continues to be used, especially in hotels where only scheme cards are accepted.

Rationalization has occurred where EFTPOS systems accepted cards with and without a PIN based on card type. The credit card issuers moved to supporting PINs on their cards for cash withdrawals from ATMs. This facilitated PINs being accepted at EFTPOS. It is interesting that for markets where PINs are commonly used, their introduction for credit cards was generally not resisted. In fact, PINs as a generalization, with no scientific proof, seem to be preferred over the use of a signature by cardholders.

A feature, or disadvantage depending on your disposition, is that proprietary debit cards support non-repudiation of the payment. No chargeback support means the card transaction is as if cash were used. If there is a dispute arising from a purchase, the cardholder has to rely either on their card issuer (bank) or an independent judicator, such as a commerce commissioner or banking ombudsman or a lawyer to achieve an acceptable resolution.

Card schemes have retained chargeback rights (repudiation), almost using this as a weapon in controlling their now clients, issuers and acquirers. This is known by the industry as the 'liability shift'.

Technical variation

An enabler of interchange and national switches was the acceptance and implementation of the ISO8583 messaging standard and related protocols across both ATM and EFTPOS, and by the card schemes. A common protocol, at least by the networks, supports the concept of interoperability. Other standards relating specifically to security are also commonly applied.

A significant point of difference is dual messaging versus single messaging. Dual messaging consists of online authorizations followed by their associated financial message, forwarded in a batch file for settlement. Single message is authorization and, if approved, a real-time posting of the debit to the cardholder's account. There are no batch settlement files. Note that many legacy retail-banking systems do not have the capability to support real-time account updates. This simply means the approved single message transactions need to be stored for end-of-day processing. Inter-day approvals need to access the stored transactions to calculate an accurate available funds balance. A bank's front-end processor must have the facility to support this processing requirement.

ATM and proprietary debit card EFTPOS are now almost universally single message. Scheme cards for EFTPOS are generally dual messaging, although Visa does support single message for EFTPOS, which apparently is only used by very few customers.

Merchants are rarely paid even when messaging is in real-time. Merchant settlement may be overnight, but for scheme cards delayed settlement is often the norm. A business justification is probably based on when the acquirer actually receives payment.

Why use dual messaging? No obvious reason, but possibly because dual replicates the original manual processing method and that is the way it has always been done. A single message network has to be built with more resilience in that cardholders' accounts are being debited. If the transaction does not complete, a reversal process needs to ensure the financial transaction, and debit is reversed. An authorization only messaging system, if not matched to a financial transaction, will, after a certain time period, drop off the system, releasing the funds that were being held.

Dual messaging will manage pre-authorizations in a more suitable manner. Pre-authorizations are used, for example, by hotels and self-service fuel dispensers.

Card rebranding

The last major event has been the re-branding of the original ATM cards. The proprietary debit cards, if branded, are now known as scheme debit cards. Proprietary cards are still surviving in many markets, such as specific purpose cards or cards linked to specific market segments.

EFTPOS and the associated debit cards have been at the forefront of the development of the cashless society. The introduction of mass transit stored value cards and, more recently, the tap and go cards for lower value transactions (without PIN) supported by the card schemes, could be argued as driving the concept of a cashless society, from being a strategic objective to being reality. There are countries now where you can survive without cash. I live in one and rarely carry cash and if I am given cash it becomes an inconvenience. What do you do with it? Normally, spend it as quickly as possible or simply throw it in your desk drawer.

EFTPOS took time to be accepted by merchants and bank customers. Banks may have expected that EFTPOS acceptance would be similar to ATMs but that was not the case. I am not sure anybody really knows why. The challenge was, in part, the requirement to convince merchants to install POS devices. Merchants were not keen to pay for the service so in many countries devices were provided at no cost to the merchant and transaction fees were not charged. This made it extremely expensive for banks. There was also the logistics involved in building the physical network.

As with many payment services there is an activity threshold or market penetration level that must be exceeded before success is assured. As with all payment services it was a transaction threshold that began to deliver the economies of scale to support a drive to delivering EFTPOS to all retailers.

A defined strategy of targeting high turnover and frequently visited retail chains such as fuel outlets and supermarkets proved successful. This was important as consumers could rely on these chains to accept EFTPOS payments and carrying cash was not a necessity.

Further cash out at EFTPOS in selective countries was also introduced to allow retailers to reduce their cash holdings. This gave retailers/merchants a positive business proposition.

For retailers, there were well-defined benefits relating to the minimization of cash holdings on their premises. An added incentive delivered by banks (and encouraged by central banks) was to charge businesses a cash-handling fee. So cash out minimizes this fee.

In the early 1990s, I implemented an EDC service for the ANZ bank in New Zealand, which was a copy of the service implemented in Australia. This service only accepted credit cards but proved so successful that securing a supply of devices to meet the retailers' demand was a significant issue. Retailers were paying for their devices through a leasing arrangement. The retailer benefit was that the system replaced both paper vouchers and the need to ring the authorization centres for approvals on transactions above their floor limit. The retailer/merchant proposition was strong, based on improving the efficiency of the payment process, allowing sales staff to be more productive (increased sales revenue), reducing the 'Friction'.

In a short period the EFTPOS payment service replaced this EDC service. However, EDC, for those that could source a device, did deliver the benefits of electronic card-based payments.

Eventually, as is the case today, a retailer must have EFTPOS for both debit and credit cards. For countries with high EFTPOS acceptance levels, shoppers simply do not carry cash.

The high transaction volume has driven down the per transaction cost.

EFTPOS today and into the future

EFTPOS is a mature payment delivery channel globally. The most significant development has been the introduction of EMV. EMV bought three significant EFTPOS service improvements:

- PIN validation on chip, enabling cardholder authentication for those networks still relying on a signature.
- Tap and go services combined with no PIN entry for lower value transactions, making payments more frictionless.
- It addressed the card fraud issue for card-present transactions.

In a number of countries, especially Australia, with tap and go, the minimum value limit for a transaction has been removed or reduced significantly and this has meant cash can more easily be replaced. In Australia, a visit to the café for a caffeine fix always used to require a visit to the ATM first; not now it seems.

There has been the development and integration of a range of newer devices. Tap and go has been supported in mass transit for many years but this has been extended to cover scheme cards. Parking meters, once only accepting coins, now accept a card for payment. To be a profitable merchant, you must have a payment card acceptance device.

The next real shift will occur if real-time payments (RTPs) are introduced as a payment option in the traditional card-present space. This will occur if there is a drive to introducing a greater level of frictionless payment. This could be done by using QR codes (as per the Alipay model) and the ISO20022 messaging standard.

The integration of POS and mobile has allowed for smaller or lower volume, mobile merchants to accept cards. My ANZ-supplied POS device supports a PIN pad, card swipe and a smart card reader, fitting onto the back of my mobile handset connected to the audio port.

This is just one example of EFTPOS development. Going forward, more of this type of development will continue.

There has been development at the point of sale, such as self-checkout at supermarkets, but this has not lead to the payment process changing. It is a new retail technology platform integrated (connected) to the existing payment process.

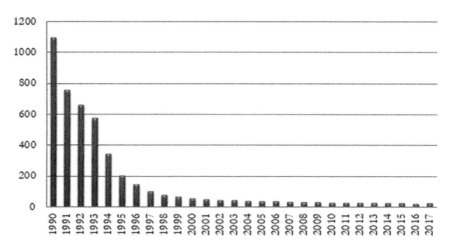

FIGURE 5.6   Inhabitants per POS device – Australia

Source: Data from Reserve Bank of Australia Statistics C8.

Figure 5.6 shows the penetration of POS devices based on people per device in the Australian market.

In 1990, there was one device for every 1100 Australians, increasing to one device for every 26 in 2017. The penetration of POS into the Australian market must be almost at saturation. Other, developed payment markets will be in a similar position but perhaps not so extreme.

Projection

EFTPOS or POS should be seen in two parts, the network, often referred to as the rails, and the point of acceptance or merchant customer (cardholder) interface.

We are seeing incremental changes in the point of acceptance space and generally these changes have not impacted the rails. EMV has not had any impact on the rails (apart from changes to message formats to support EMV-related data) nor has tap and go. Devices themselves will continue to develop. The focus will remain on reducing the friction and retaining/improving the trust (security).

The next major change will involve moving away from ISO8583 and the adoption of ISO20022. This will facilitate two capability improvements:

- Transportation of enriched data through the POS networks (rails).
- RTP payments from buyer to seller using a mobile type device.

The latter could be supported through the existing ISO8583 standard but it will not deliver the enriched data that retailers and marketers seem so desperate to acquire. I am not sure the average consumer will be so keen for marketers to have the capability of profiling based on the content of their shopping basket.

Refer to the section entitled 'Messaging standard ISO20022' in Chapter 6.

Card issuers will be able to provide individual cardholders, whether businesses or individuals, with a breakdown of their spending. This – especially for businesses – should meet a need.

We may see consumers using a mobile handset app to scan bar codes of products they have selected. On finishing the selection process the app generates a RTP message for the total value and forwards a payment approval message to the checkout. Handset scanning allows the consumer to pass through checkout.

This process may not be more frictionless for the purchaser; however, it is a winner for the merchant. If implemented using ISO20022 the merchant will receive all the purchasing details required by their back office system plus some highly valued customer data.

Cards and card schemes

I once referred to a payment card as an access control device and, with the arrival of EMV, it is more so than back when I used that term. Fundamentally, it identifies the cardholder and enables the linking of the cardholder to their profile, permissions and accounts. The card also holds the security elements to authenticate the cardholder.

A card's plastic/chip is also referred to as a form factor. The mobile phone is an alternative form factor. There is also the concept of a virtual card. This is where no plastic is issued but a card number is allocated to enable online payments, often in the prepaid card space.

How should we categorize the card schemes, particular Visa and MasterCard? The Visa and MasterCard networks (the card rails) are supporting the interchange of transactions between their participants. The card is not issued by the schemes; the transactions are not acquired by the schemes and the accounts being accessed are managed outside of the scheme domain. They support payments between financial institutions that have no relationship, except both are scheme participants.

Essentially, Visa and MasterCard are traditional networks with a strong brand. They jealously protect and heavily promote their brands. They utilize a pull strategy where cardholders who are not their direct customers are encouraged to use a card carrying their brand. The card sub-brands of gold, platinum, etc., are about assigning cardholders a status supporting their card issuer to deliver value added services for a larger card fee.

Since incorporation, the schemes have attempted to expand their scope of influence but essentially they are still a network, the card rails. Their business model is still built on the number of cards on issue generating transaction volume. Fundamentally, by increasing the card base, the transactions will follow with a push marketing strategy. The fee structure has supported this business model and these organizations spend big dollars on their brand image.

What has always been of interest and amazes me is that the schemes are almost disinterested in the merchant side of their business, except when it comes to fraudulent activities, which of course threaten their brand. The underlying premise is, if buyers of goods and services insist on paying by card then merchants have no option but to accept cards.

Each of the schemes will at times work with a large retail organization or large merchant to promote usage. The Singapore (national) sale has been an excellent example of this type of activity.

Card system processing model

The card systems have been built on the request and response model. This is where the payee (merchant) initiates the payment by requesting an approval to accept the payer's payment instrument (card). A paper/manual-based model was computerized but not changed as the process remains the same.

Figure 5.7 illustrates the request and response model.

The card system model has been transitioned into an electronic form but never re-engineered. Progressively computerized over multiple decades; the model has been patched and built to serve an evolving payment landscape.

The request and response model is open to attack by fraudsters. In this payment model, the merchant needs to know the payer's payment instrument details. If the payment details are recorded and hacked then fraudulent payments can be generated by fraudsters acting as legitimate payees until the payer or issuer/acquirer discover the fraud.

To address this we now have the following list of anti-fraud elements, developed and implemented over 30+ years:

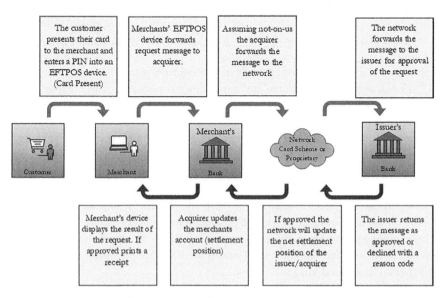

FIGURE 5.7 Request and response model

- PINs and PIN block security
- CVV1
- CVV2
- EMV
- PCI
- Virtual cards
- Tokens
- Data encryption
- 3D secure
- Risk management software

This list can be expected to continue growing.

Has the request and response model, as deployed by the card payment sector, reached its end of life with the RTP networks increasingly being implemented into the traditional card markets? On the positive side, this model has served the payments industry well and will continue for some time into the future just because it is firmly entrenched.

Card types

The card types supported by the schemes have expanded over the last few decades for various reasons. Schemes traditionally supported revolving credit but now support prepaid, gift and debit cards. There is little that distinguishes these card types within the scheme domain. For card issuers, they are distinctly different card types (or products).

A credit card product based on unsecured lending just does not work in many less developed countries. Countries where personal lending is not well established often do not have the supporting services, such as a credit bureau, to enable credit scoring. Offering a credit card, a generic unsecured lending product, carries a high risk to the lender in these countries.

For the Russian situation in the 1990s, we came up with the positive balance credit card. Cardholders were required to hold security (collateral) against their credit card account. The bank could use this collateral to cover any unpaid amounts owing. Back then we had the issue of merchant floor limits so cardholders while travelling could exceed their credit limits, which did not become apparent until the transactions were cleared. The collateral was the solution to deal with this situation.

Back then we did not have card scheme debit cards and connecting to the customers' accounts for funds checking was probably not feasible. ^aA story was told about a branch manager near the Arctic Circle who held all her customers account balances in her head. She wrote them on slate for a back-up.^b

Debit cards

The card that started off in many markets as the ATM card, was accepted at the point of sale and is now generally referred to simply as the proprietary debit card, provides access to accounts managed by the issuing bank's retail banking system. Accounts are required to be classified as deposit accounts. It is also worth remembering that in many developing economies banks do not operate retail-banking systems that are available 24/7 for authorizations so the debit card account may be managed in an alternative system. One may refer to these as reloadable prepaid cards.

A significant view of credit cards is that they are generally considered as a payment instrument used for higher value transactions. Available statistics support this fact. During a period of economic stagnation – or austerity, as is the modern term – credit card usage also stagnates, which impacts card scheme revenue. The card schemes, in effect, saw the banks' proprietary debit cards as their competition and a card product that was more resilient to economic fluctuations. Debit cards are used to pay for the essentials of life.

The card schemes, by introducing their own scheme debit card brand and promoting it to their issuing banks as a replacement for their proprietary debit card, not only increased their transaction volumes but also provided a defence against periods of economic stagnation.

Banks have been supportive of scheme-branded debit cards for a number of reasons:

- In many cases banks did not charge merchant fees on debit and in a few countries banks paid the merchants for accepting their proprietary debit cards. Scheme branding of debit cards allowed banks to earn interchange revenue, recovering the lost revenue on credit cards due to regulator intervention.
- The banks proprietary debit cards came under scheme rules/processes enabling them to be accepted for e-commerce purchases, again increasing the revenue from these cards, and a pragmatist may say 'also the fraud'.
- Banks, by supporting a scheme debit card, which is accessing a deposit account, could counter competitive pressure from the independent prepaid card issuers.

The only losers are perhaps the merchants, although in various countries they have been able to negotiate a lower blended merchant discount fee.

Prepaid cards

These cards are usually issued for a specific purpose and accepted in a closed loop network. They can be scheme branded, enabling them to be accepted where credit and debit cards are accepted. Essentially they are cards that can be reloaded as required, either at kiosks, through a direct debit to a bank account or a reoccurring payment from a credit or debit card.

The most prominent prepaid cards are found in the mass transit sector, such as Oyster in the UK, Octopus in Hong Kong and Ez-Link in Singapore. Today, virtually every city with a transit system has a prepaid proximity card. From a conceptual view, the transit card is an upgraded ten trip ticket, or a token purchased for a larger sum of money that entitles travel for an extended period such as a month or, as I had many years ago in Melbourne, 12 months.

The key point here is that less efficient non-electronic payment services have been replaced with an efficient electronic payment method. The mindset change for the transit user has been kept to a minimum and adoption has generally been rapid or often simply enforced.

Prepaid cards are normally not personalized except if automatic reload is supported from a card or bank account.

The mass transit operators in some countries are moving into the general retail space for lower value purchases. The card schemes' tap and go (NFC) deployment may be considered a response to this threat. We are also seeing scheme cards being accepted by the mass transit operators, the rationale for this is based on cost. The cost of accepting a bank-issued and -maintained card is less than supporting a proprietary mass transit card, especially if the regulators are driving down the merchant fees. In addition, mass transit operators have volume like no one else, so can negotiate lower fees.

Accepting a scheme card is also more convenient for the casual mass transit user.

Gift cards

Another existing product, gift vouchers, has been replaced by the payment card. Gift cards are normally purchased with a set value, are not rechargeable and not personalized. There can always the exceptions, and rechargeable gift cards can be found, but then I would consider such cards prepaid.

For the issuer, who is normally a retailer, possibly using a service provider, unused balances are claimed to be a significant income source.

Charge cards

The concept of a charge card has been around a long time and for many large retailers this card is today's upgraded proprietary charge account. American Express's primary product is a charge card fitting into this space, and could be referred to as a scheme card.

A charge card is normally considered one where the full balance is paid off on a due date. Free credit is provided on all transactions for the current payment period, normally a month.

The charge card schemes such as American Express and Discovery/Diners Club have consistently targeted the business or corporate sector and the merchants who also target this sector. Their merchant discount rates have also traditionally been higher than Visa and MasterCard.

Although the ground has shifted over recent years it is probably still valid to describe the charge card schemes as not four but three pillars, with the scheme rather than the banks owning the cardholder (not necessarily always) and merchant relationships.

Concluding comment

The distinction between card types is becoming increasingly blurred as issuers define their card products to better fit the market segment being targeted.

The card simply provides access to the cardholder's available funds or credit facility to purchase goods and services in a closed or open payment network.

Card usage trends

Yearly transaction volume

Figure 5.8 provides a transaction comparison between debit and credit (inclusive of charge) for the UK. The dominance of debit is obvious.

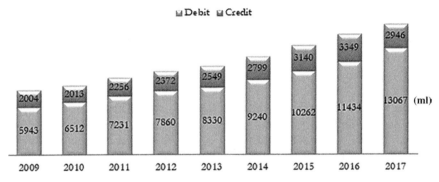

FIGURE 5.8   Credt/debit card transaction (ml) comparison – UK

Source: Data from Finance UK Statistics (UK Card Association).

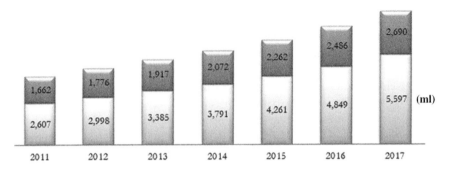

FIGURE 5.9   Credit/debit card transaction (ml) comparison – Australia

Source: Card data from Reserve Bank of Australia Statistics C1 & C5.

This figure illustrates the separation between the growth of the two systems, even post the Global Financial Crisis (GFC).

Travel to almost the other side of the world from the UK and you will find a similar outcome in Australia.

The Australian market, because of its size has more seasonal fluctuations, with spending picking up each year in the summer months. However, debit, which has always been strong in this market since its introduction in the 1980s, is increasingly out growing credit.

Figure 5.9 is a comparison and is sourced from data provided by the Reserve Bank of Australia, which I have always found to be the most comprehensive and therefore useful.

There is a unique concept in this market where a single card (plastic) will support access to multiple accounts and account selection by the cardholder determines the card type – credit or debit.

Other influences driving card trends

For the card industry, while we see a continued growth on card usage, whether debit or credit, there is a reduction in the average ticket size. The average value in the UK in 2010 for debit was £44.56 and credit £63.78, but in 2016 the average value had dropped to £40.81 and £55.65 respectively.

The rationale for this is the introduction of contactless (tap and go) acceptance. In 2009, contactless had 0 per cent of the UK market but by 2015 its share had risen to 12 per cent. In 2016 contactless growth rate over the previous year soared by 178 per cent. Contactless is aligned with lower value transactions and you might rightly say its introduction should not impact credit card transaction values. Cardholders, known as transactors, will use credit credits for all their transactions regardless of value.

In GBP, the spending in 2016 was for debit cards £40.6 billion compared with credit cards at £16.0 billion with a growth rate of 5 per cent and 2.4 per cent, respectively.

The UK Card Association also made the claim that in 2006 payment cards had 55 per cent market share of retail business, with cash and cheques at 45 per cent. By 2015 the payment cards share had shot up to 78.5 per cent. This is further evidence of the cashless and cheque-less society is upon us.

The latest MasterCard Digital Purchasing Survey (Sydney, 15 March 2017) stated that more than four in five (82 per cent) of Australians are using tap and go to make payments every week. Further 33 per cent of Australians are annoyed if a merchant does not support tap and go. I am one of these.

The rationale is apparently convenience, and the security issue according to MasterCard has been receding. Australians are perhaps trading any security concerns (trust) for convenience (reduced friction).

However, any preference for mobile phones over plastic as the form factor is apparently not being seen. Maybe cardholders are not fully aware of the mobile option.

Card fraud

Fraud has become all-consuming for the payments industry and in particular for card not present (CNP).

The European Central Bank, *Fourth Report on Card Fraud*, July 2015 contains 2013 data, which is a little dated. However, the trends illustrated in this report are continuing. In 2013, fraud on cards issued within the Single Euro Payments Area (SEPA) and acquired globally was €1.44 billion (0.039 per cent of the total transaction value), split 66 per cent CNP, 20 per cent EFTPOS and 14 per cent ATMs.

Card present fraud is declining, attributed to the adoption of EMV. Fraud is expected to decline even further as countries outside of SEPA adopt EMV. Fraudsters have switched their efforts onto card not present (e-commerce).

The report stated that 2 per cent of transactions acquired outside of SEPA accounted for 22 per cent of the fraud. This contributed to the use of magnetic stripe in countries where security standards are lower (EMV not fully adopted).

The *Financial Fraud Action UK – Fraud The Facts 2017* publication provides more up-to-date UK payment statistics. These statistics are consistent with the SEPA view and clearly illustrate the size of the problem and the trends.

Figure 5.10 clearly illustrates the growth in Remote Purchase Fraud (CNP) on UK issued cards.

Consistent with the SEPA statements is the decline in counterfeit fraud (card present) in contrast to CNP fraud. Chip and PIN (EMV) will claim the credit for this decline. A factor in CNP fraud is also the growth in e-commerce.

Figure 5.11 illustrates the split between fraud committed on UK cards in-country as opposed to abroad.

The interesting factor here is that the two trends have followed each other with UK fraud increasing marginally over time. In 2007, the percentage split was 61/39 (UK/Abroad) whereas by 2016 it was 68/32.

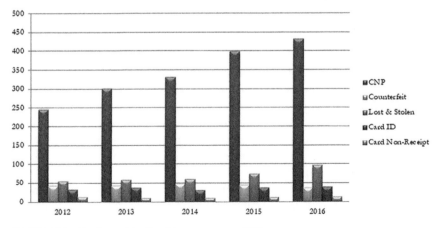

FIGURE 5.10 Card trend in fraud by category – UK

Source: Data from *Financial Fraud Action UK (GBP ml) – Fraud the Facts 2017*

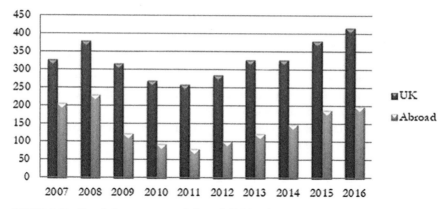

FIGURE 5.11   Fraud, in-country and abroad (GBP ml) – UK issued cards

Source: Data from *Financial Fraud Action UK – Fraud the Facts 2017.*

Card fraud to monitor

The *Financial Fraud Action UK – Fraud The Facts 2017* publication illustrates a dramatic increase in lost and stolen card fraud, as illustrated in Figure 5.12.

The reason is not fully explained by Financial Fraud Action UK but they do mention contactless cards. However, they infer only a small amount of fraud can be contributed to these cards. It is true that the contactless or tap and go transactions are restricted in value. The specific amount is set at the country level.

The UK Card Association has been quoted as claiming that contactless fraud for 2016 was £7 million or 0.032 per cent. This figure is only marginally better than the card fraud level quoted by the European Central Bank for all cards issued within SEPA. That percentage was 0.039 per cent.

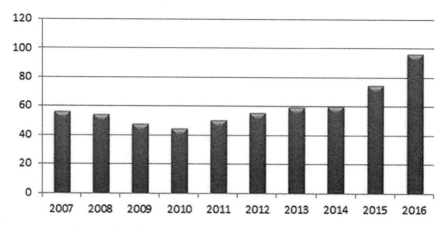

FIGURE 5.12   Lost and stolen card fraud (GBP ml) – UK

Source: Data from *Financial Fraud Action UK – Fraud the Facts 2017.*

Online banking fraud

Not specifically card connected but of interest is online banking fraud. This is connected to identify theft. Financial Fraud Action UK reports, for 2016, 20,088 cases with a total value of £101.8 million or approximately £5068 per case. For 2015 the number of cases was marginally lower at 19,691 and the total value was £133.5 million or approximately £6780 per case.

This is the fraud I expect to become problematic as PTM-based payments and banking services become more widely used.

Efforts to combat fraud

The industry has made a considerable effort to address the security issues. There are two fundamental reasons:

- The cost of fraud.
- Citizen confidence in the system.

Although the first is measurable and investment in fraud can be measured on ROI, confidence in the system is a more critical issue. If confidence (trust) is lost, citizens will look for alternatives such as reverting to cash or possibly considering new unregulated payment services such as represented by cryptocurrencies (a future option).

Key measures taken

Efforts taken to combat fraud have been discussed separately but they need to be viewed holistically.

In the early years of electronic payments, security was largely algorithm based. Data were viewed as either:

- sensitive and needing to be encrypted, specifically PIN blocks, or
- protected against being changed either purposely or accidently.

Encryption is based on the DES (now 3DES) algorithm. Protection was achieved by the generation of a Message Authentication Code (MAC).

Encryption is enhanced by using dynamic keys. This approach is based on exchanging new keys usually at time intervals or after x transactions, where x can be 1 if that is the requirement.

MACs traditionally have been based on block ciphers such as DES. Hash-based MACs using a secret key in conjunction with a cryptographic hash function have become the preferred approach.

MACs were often generated by software, which is less secure so using a HSM (Hardware Security Module) is a far more secure approach.

Utilizing PKI (Public Key Infrastructure), messages can be digitally signed. This is an asymmetric key structure where each party has a key pair; one is private and other public. The data encrypted using one key must be decrypted using the other key. If the sender encrypts using their private key and then re-encrypts using the receiver's public key the data is signed. The receiver decrypts using their private key and then decrypts the result with the sender's public key to verify the message is, first, for them and, second, it is from a trusted source.

PKI can be used to exchange symmetric keys between parties in a secure manner.

To understand the correct method/algorithm to be used for a specific requirement, working with a data security specialist who is familiar with the payment industries standards is recommended. This specialist should also be able to advise on the best practice to manage keys.

Tokenization

Tokenization is a new approach to addressing the payment risk and is a means of reducing the impact of PCI-DSS on the acquiring side of payments. As a new approach there is a lack of standards implying a business risk to those using this method. Therefore the implementations can vary significantly.

Tokens can:

- Be numeric or alphanumeric characters.
- Look like a card number with the IIN/BIN (first six characters) excluded so the issuer can still be identified.
- Be a payment instrument in its own right in which case the merchant may not be able to distinguish a PAN from a Token.

The token is a representation in encrypted form of the card's PAN (primary account number) or simply the card number. The intent of the token is to replace the PAN. This relies on the ability not to be able to detokenize the value to derive the PAN. Further, the PAN and its token cannot coexist in the same environment, allowing for the matching of the two.

Single use tokens can be used to again add further security.

Vaults are used to enable the mapping of tokens to PANs.

The strength of any token is dependent on the strict access controls applied to the vault, plus the strength of the cryptographic algorithm used and the protection (key management regime) of the keys used to generate the tokens.

Refer to the PCI-DSS Tokenization Guidelines for an understanding of how to implement a compliant tokenization scheme.

Card mobile tokens

Tokenization is being used in the mobile wallet/NFC implementation. Holding tokens in the wallet is potentially more secure than holding PANs, especially if the token is dynamic and changes after each transaction.

With such implementations the wallet provider is required to participate in the transaction authorization process, as the custodian of the vault, to substitute the token for the PAN. If the token contains the BIN in the clear the transaction can be switched back to the issuer who then can be the vault custodian.

I have two concerns with tokenization:

- If the token is static will it be just another card number and can be exploited by the fraudsters?
- If tokens are managed by PSPs and mobile operators, are we going to see attacks similar to on-file card databases even if vaults are deployed?

Is deploying strong encryption where the keys are appropriately managed just as effective? Further, for e- and m-commerce, is not using one-time or limited-use vertical card numbers very similar?

Without doubt, tokenization is a space to watch as the technology matures and the standards are developed.

Are tokens really needed?

PCI requires that card numbers are not stored in a clear format. Tokenization as opposed to encryption is an option for particular situations such as mobile wallets.

If a merchant's EFTPOS system is not integrated with their retail point of sales system then there is no issue. This is where the retailer's point of sale system forwards a payment request to the EFTPOS device and waits for either decline or approved response. The retailer's point of sale system receives no payment card details.

The PCI issue only arises with fully integrated retailer's point-of-sale systems that connect directly to the payment network.

For mobile wallets that use tokens, the merchant has no PCI compliance issue. However, while merchants are accepting both plastic and mobile wallet form factors for payment then they are not PCI exempt.

For CNP payments, similar logic applies. If the e-commerce website passes off the payment element to a PSP who acts as a vertical EFTPOS device, then there is no PCI compliance for the merchant only for the PSP.

For businesses who store card details to support reoccurring payments then tokenization is an option, but they would also need to consider a vault. The other option is to deploy strong encryption to protect card numbers and the other details they are permitted to store. For more details see PCI DSS Quick Reference Guide Version 3.2.1, July 2018 (www.pcisecuritystandards.org/documents/PCI_DSS-QRG-v3_2_1.pdf?agreement=true&time=1540786671259).

Some may argue that to track their customers' behaviour especially if they do not have a loyalty system they need to retain card numbers. Card numbers will never show a complete view as they change and customers usually have multiple cards. For more details see the section in Chapter 3 entitled 'Big data'.

Future projection – credit cards

For the card sector participants it is all about transaction volume resulting from cards on issue. For the major card issuers it is all about debit versus credit (and charge). Of these two card types, which is dominating, which will disappear? My view is that the future is bleak for credit cards. It is rare in the payments business for a product or service to totally vanish. If this does happen, cheques will be first to disappear. The credit card will survive but not necessarily as we know it and the account structure supporting the card may change significantly. Debit and credit cards may become one.

The credit card was built on the need to have a payment instrument that would support the purchasing of goods and services, card present. It was brought to market before technology started to take over. The introduction of magnetic stripes in the 1970s was the start of the digitization of payments.

In the past:

- For purchases with a value above the merchant's floor limit, the merchant was required to contact a call centre for an approval.
- The card being embossed was placed in a zip-zap machine, a multi-leaf carbon copy paper voucher enabled an imprint to be manually taken with the sales details added and then signed by the cardholder.
- Merchants were also required to consult a bulletin of 'hot' cards to determine if they were able to accept a card.
- The acquirer's copies of the vouchers were batched at the end of day by the merchant and banked.

The process has not changed.

- Details of the payment are captured electronically.
- PINs have replaced signatures in most situations.
- Authorizations (if not tap and go) are requested electronically.
- Merchant transactions are settled in the same manner but again electronically.

In the paper-based days, a transaction could take days if not weeks to eventually be posted to the cardholder's account. I am assuming in part this is the reason for offering an interest free period to cardholders. This period was only offered to cardholders who paid the full balance of their account on or before due date. Those who paid off their accounts in full each month were labelled as transactors. Those who do not pay on the due date, taking advantage of the revolving credit facility, are referred to as revolvers.

The timing of network settlement along with the acquirers paying their merchants is not normally coordinated. Acquirers may delay paying their merchants until settlement has taken place but there should be little value in this practice today as the timing between the two should be insignificant, hours rather than days.

Issuers, however, are required to settle with the network prior to their credit cardholders paying. So, in effect, they are providing funding to the acquirers and therefore the merchants.

The argument therefore is that the credit card interest rates are high for a number of reasons, but a significant one must be to cover the interest transactors are not paying. A supporter of the current system may argue this loss of issuer income is covered by the interchange rate. That may be partially true but then there are pressures to reduce the interchange rates.

The point is, the revolvers are subsidizing transactors and I do not understand how that is a sustainable model, although it has endured for many decades. The efficiencies that technology has or can deliver have not passed fully through to the payment method's business model. This aspect of timing is a cause for reviewing the end-to-end process.

Reengineering card processing

When card processing was becoming an established payment service, the need was for 24 hours 365/6 days availability. Banks then, as many do today, have limitations on their retail banking systems' ability to stay on-line continuously all hours because of the need for a batch-processing window. Yes, they use work-arounds with store and forward files, mirroring of account balances in off-line files, etc. If not necessarily in the most elegant of ways, this problem has been resolved for debit cards.

Further retail banking systems had no capability to neither manage card issuance nor support a merchant base. As a result, card management systems supporting merchants and cardholders (including account management) were developed and deployed for credit cards. Therefore, as a general rule, credit cards operate off their own discrete processing platform from debit cards. The more up-to-date card management systems do support an integrated approach.

On the business side, credit cards are not a typical banking product. Unsecured lending has traditionally not been a space for banks to operate. The fraud risks, although in the early period of credit cards they were manageable and unsophisticated, have changed to represent a major business risk, as discussed in this book. It needs to be noted that card scheme debit cards carry the same risk.

The message protocol (ISO8583) was deployed by Visa and MasterCard for purchase transactions in a dual context. For purchases (POS) this has generally been limited to authorizations, the 01xx message types. ATMs are supported by the single or financial message, the 02xx message types.

Under a single message, all transactions are authorized and cleared in real-time. There is an argument that dual messaging should be phased out. Dual may be seen as more appropriate for transactions requiring a pre-approval, but these can be handled under a single message system.

There is also an argument that card messaging should migrate to ISO20022, also discussed in this book refer to 'Messaging standard ISO20022' in Chapter 6.

My view is that Card issuers will look to shift away from a product (credit card) that only attracts adverse press coverage and is high maintenance in terms of managing cardholders. Pressure by regulators resulting from lobbying by merchant and cardholder groups is resulting in pressure to constrain interest rates and fees. Therefore, why not just roll credit cards up into the retail product line? Drop the term 'credit card' and utilize the debit card platform. A single card platform with cards linked to accounts with lines of credit supports both casual purchases and instalment purchases, which may have interest-free periods funded by the merchant.

Change could be introduced gradually and unobtrusively without impacting cardholders. Statistics clearly show cardholder preferences for debit cards.

Risk management systems

All EFT switching systems and authorization modules of card management (or front-end switching) systems will undertake some low-level checks based on limits and velocity. These are more to manage cardholder delinquency than fraud.

To manage fraud, there has been significant development in transaction-based risk assessment systems. These systems look at each transaction and generate a risk score. Based on the score action is taken.

The most common systems are rule-based but there are neural systems available as well. For most card issuers, the decision on type and level of sophistication to deploy is based on the size of their card base and level of fraud they are experiencing.

The options are based on either:

- rules or neural,
- inline or delayed (post approval).

Rule-based systems are based on known fraudulent activity. Card issuers and acquirers within a market will often cooperate closely when it comes to fraud. When one experiences a new attack they will pass this on to their colleagues in the other financial institutions so they can implement a new rule. If one institution experiences a new attack the others can also expect to experience this same attack so cooperation benefits all and it is a non-competitive space.

Neural systems generally also support rules but are also capable of machine learning and predictive analytics to identify a new threat as it occurs.

Inline systems (real-time), where the transaction is assessed during the approval process, will decline transactions with a high score. Many systems only do the assessment post approval (near real-time). Issuers generally do not wish to decline a payment request without first referring to the cardholder. A transaction with a high score may still be a valid payment request and a decline will inconvenience the cardholder unnecessarily.

Transactions (cases) judged to be a threat but not declined in real-time are scored, prioritized and queued to a specific fraud officer based on the score. Fraud officers with the greatest level of experience would normally receive the cases with the highest scores. Officers will investigate each case and may contact the cardholder for verification of the transaction's legitimacy. Cases that are proved fraudulent are flagged and the system should automatically generate a chargeback.

Again, based on size and the level of fraud, each institution will decide whether they operate a 24-hour, 7 day-a-week fraud investigation desk or limit it to cover the busiest daily period, as well as basing it on when cardholders can be contacted.

Smart (chip) cards

The Micro Circuit Card or Chip Card or Smart Card, whichever name you prefer, was a technology solution that was going to change payments. However, we soon viewed the chip as a solution looking for a problem.

I was first introduced to smart cards in the late 1980s and, for a very short time, I was my country's representative to a Paris-based organization that was developing the standards for microcircuit cards. This organization handed over its responsibilities to ISO shortly after my involvement – but not because of my involvement.

Smart cards was the first payments technology that captured the interest of the IT industry to a level not dissimilar to what we are experiencing with the current FinTech phenomena.

The chip was to contain all our personal information. Such as your citizen or ID card, assuming your country issued such a card, hold your medical records, be your bank card, a stored value purse, provide access to buildings/offices, your coffee loyalty points, and so on.

A number of closed loop smart card schemes were developed. MasterCard released press statements in the 1990s that all their cards would become chip enabled. Visa, to counter this initiative, announced they were developing, in partnership with a Japanese IT company, a smart card with a screen and key board.

The chip card essentially failed to meet our expectations, but all was not negative.

Mass transit

As mentioned earlier, the technology solution that solved the mass transit prepaid card problem was the chip card. The mass transit systems are closed loop, each developed to specifically meet the needs of the individual transit schemes. With the card's integration with a host system, complex fare structures could be developed to support daily commuters using multiple transit services. As an example, to discourage citizens from entering the city centres, 'park and ride' fares were able to be offered to commuters.

A common requirement for mass transit was the speed of the payment process. Card presentment was contactless and the operating system supported minimal security elements. Sony's FeliCa chips have been used in many deployments and we are now seeing mobile NFC becoming available.

NFC-enabled scheme cards are also starting to be accepted at mass transit gates where the cardholders' debit or credit account is debited in real-time. London and Singapore are two examples of where this is happening.

It may be that mass transit saves the mobile wallet.

Examples of typical projects

Mondex

Mondex, a MasterCard product, was going to become a stored value smart card. Using today's terminology a smart card wallet replacing cash with no real audit trail covering transactions. Pilots were launched and various banks signed up around the globe, and then it disappeared.

Multos a multi-application operating system and the Multos Consortium was the outcome of Mondex. Multos is the operating system used on MasterCard's EMV cards.

Business travel card

In the 1990s, the Savings Bank of the Russian Federation purchased a licence for the South African NET 1 stored value system. SBRF's need was based on supporting the cash requirements of their customers travelling within Russia. Although the bank had a national network of branches, at the time they did not have an efficient method of authorizing cash withdrawals from an account held at another branch. Travellers needed to carry a large amount of cash, which had inherent security risks.

The solution was deployed so travellers could load value onto their cards prior to travelling and then access the funds at bank branches. The card, at least initially, could not be used at merchants. All transactions originated within the SBRF branch network.

Smart City

Also during the same period, I met an American/Irish stored value solution, called Smart City, that was being implemented by a Russian oil company. In 1997 I came across Smart City again while on contract to ICL in the United Kingdom. Working with an ICL employee and ex-Unisys colleague (Andrew Neil) we were charged with the establishment of a payments business unit. Andrew and I discovered ICL had been contracted to develop parts of the Smart City system but the Irish company who had contracted ICL went bankrupt. ICL was never paid but still had the source code. Teaming up with an American business, which was in a similar position who had also developed components of Smart City, a strategy was developed and executed.

Smart City was typical of the smart card payment systems at that time. The technology was propriety and operated as a closed loop. The business model was built on the needs of campuses, whether industrial, educational or military. Smart City had been installed on a US warship. The whole intent of these implementations was to remove cash from a closed environment, to essentially address the cash management challenges related to crime and fraud.

The mobile wallet

Is the mobile wallet another fantasy of the technologists or will it take-off? Wallets are reported to be struggling but as a mobile wallet holder I do believe they have a future but need to overcome a few barriers.

These being:

- for all points of acceptance to support NFC,
- support for a full range of cards in each domestic market.

All points of acceptance – NFC capable

Each domestic market will take time to have all POS devices supporting NFC because of the various ownership arrangements. If merchants are leasing their device(s) they may be locked into their current device unable to upgrade. Merchants who own their devices will want to write down the book value of their existing devices. If a bank owns the devices then upgrading maybe quicker if the business case is supportive.

As we have seen, existing devices may support a NFC peripheral device.

The fortunate factor is that NFC is not only a mobile phone feature with the technology originally introduced to support contactless cards, and tap-go acceptance. Travelling through Europe, NFC is supported at all types of points of acceptance, broader than just traditional retailers, particularly transport and parking.

One wallet all cards

The sales pitch for the mobile wallet has been, 'leave home with only your phone'. The various wallets are, to varying degrees, able to fulfil this goal. My bank's wallet definitely does not. However, when I look at all the cards in my wallet I do not believe this goal is achievable yet. I have cards with a chip, cards with no chip, and cards with QR codes only and then there are my driving licences. All these card issuers, as I understand it, will need to sign up to a wallet provider(s).

Only when all cards are loaded can I dispense with my physical wallet. If I have to open my physical wallet for one card I might as well do so for all cards. It is simpler and quicker. The only time I can leave my wallet at home is if I am visiting my local convenience store that has an NFC POS device.

We are seeing mobile card storage for all these other card types (images) but this is supported by a separate application. This is not really a solution although it may allow the physical wallet to stay at home.

Each market is different and what citizens have in their wallet is different. Therefore, wallets need to be localized and what comes from the tech giants is unlikely to recognize this fact. A generic product and service needs to be set-up to meet local conditions, which means certified local providers should manage the process where they work with all the card issuers, whether payment, loyalty, etc., and whether they are scheme or proprietary. Standards must be adhered to for interoperability, domestic and international.

I kind of trust my bank; it has known me for years and has never overtly used the information it has on me. My bank has never sold my data, along with any other customers' data, for profit or any other reason. Certified local wallet providers would have to demonstrate the same level of integrity.

The Reserve Bank of Australia has a stated objective to drive down interchange rates. If the RBA is consistent in having fees transparent to bank customers, a wallet transaction fee like the ATM fee may need to be directly charged to the subscriber, at the time of completing the transaction. This is adding friction as well as direct cardholder cost.

Is there too much reliance on the mobile handset and does this expose all of us? This was discussed in Chapter 2.

Projections – cards

There is enormous scope for creativity with respect to developing a payment card product. The fuel card industry is one where I have recently seen a very complex card offering, one even the issuer didn't fully understand because, over the years, they built too much complexity into their product offering. Many card products do not neatly fit into the boxes of debit, credit, prepaid, etc.

Scheme branding offers the card issuer global acceptance. Not all issuers will qualify for scheme branding and card acceptance will be vanilla outside of the issuers' managed environment. Scheme branding also comes at a cost, which for small issuers cannot be justified even if they qualify.

Everything seems to follow a circular pattern so we might begin to see more proprietary card products being introduced, targeted at the needs of specific communities. Private labelling may see a rebirth. This does not necessarily provide domestic or global acceptance, so the more generic card scheme products will survive.

Debit cards will be the product that underpins the card schemes' business models and deliver growth. Credit cards for the schemes will have good and bad years based on the economic conditions within each cardholder's home market. The card schemes will look for growth in non-traditional markets with probably little short-term success. They need to play a long game.

CNP fraud will continue to be a work in progress until a truly effective solution is found.

Mobile wallets, I suspect, may be one of those technologies that we in a decade may say, 'do you remember when…'.

The distinction between card types is becoming increasingly blurred as issuers define their card products to better fit the market segments they are targeting. Potentially, cardholders should be able to define their own product within a set of parametrized features to allow high net worth bank customers to have their individual needs satisfied.

I recently sat through a vendor presentation of a middle-ware software product that was promoting the capability of tailoring card products to specific individuals or small groups of cardholders, so the potential to support this requirement is available.

Real-Time Payments

Near Real-Time Payments are often referred to as simply Real-Time Payments (RTPs) or Faster Payments after the United Kingdom service.

RTP services are reported to be operational in Japan, Switzerland, Brazil, Mexico, the UK and Singapore. In addition, to this list needs to be added Bahrain, the service I assisted in the design and vendor/solution selection, drafted the operational rulebook plus developed the fee model. Countries working on services are SEPA in Europe for cross-border payments; Feds in the USA have established a task force and Australia has launched the National Payments Platform (NPP).

RTP payment systems are essentially built on the Pay Away or Buyer Initiated Payment model. Others may refer to this model as push payments. RTP systems optionally may support a request to pay instructions sent by the payee. The instruction should contain the payees' payment details so the payer can respond simply by accepting the request with a RTP payment request (Pay Away). The request to pay is not a financial message.

Typically, a RTP service should process direct credits and debits, bill presentments and faster payments.

The payer's bank is responsible for validating the instruction, ensuring there are sufficient funds in the payer's account before forwarding the credit instruction to the payee's bank. The payee's bank may reject the instruction primarily if the account number is invalided or the account has been closed.

Potentially there may be an anti-money laundering (AML) reason to reject a payment by either bank. This will be based on unusual activity on either account that the respective bank has identified.

Pay Away payments are not exclusive to RTP services, such payment instructions are processed through batch clearing and settlement services, often referred to as direct credits. A payroll payment is a direct credit and a Pay Away instruction.

RTP is where the focus is today, although I do not see batch processing disappearing in the short term. Where time is not critical and the settlement risk is of no concern then the traditional monolithic processes will remain in the medium term because of their inherent processing efficiency, resulting in lower per payment instruction cost. However, the longer-term future will see changes. Traditional batch transactions will be processed through RTP services on delayed bases as single transactions, possibly overnight to utilize unutilized capacity in non-peak processing periods.

Launching a RTP system with the intent that it will replace the existing end-of-day batch processes also facilitates the introduction of the ISO20022 standard in a non-disruptive manner. Shoehorning a new messaging standard into an old, poorly document software, developed using 1980s or earlier methods is a recipe for disaster. Using today's standards in a new system, build with a view to the future, without having to make critical compromises, is the only sensible approach.

RTP processing model

Figure 5.13 illustrates the Pay Away method.

The alternative card-processing model is referred to as request and response.

RTP expectations

The expectation is that RTP services will radically change the payment landscape is indicated by strong user (personal and business) support. The payment types being impacted are:

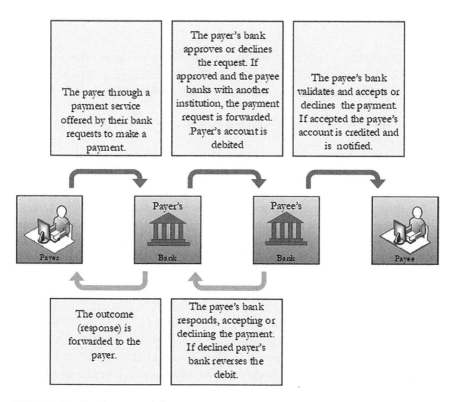

FIGURE 5.13 Pay Away model

- Immediate internet-based person-to-person payments.
- Immediate bill and other payments (C2B, B2B and B2C) reducing the load on ACH systems.
- Small businesses not only paying their bills in real-time but also their staff wages.
- A potential primary payment method for e-commerce transactions replacing card not present (CNP) payments.

Although RTP can be – and in specific markets will be – delivered through Smart ATMs, the prime delivery channel will be through the PTM (PC, Tablet and Mobile phones) platform.

The RTP (Pay-Away) model's advantages over the card payment model, referred to as request and response, are:

- Efficient and inherently more secure.
- Payers are authenticated and the payment is approved before entering the payment network.
- The number of declines and reversals required to be handled by the network is significantly reduced.
- Merchants (payees) are not required to request and process payer's payment details.

The Australian Service NPP (New Payment Platform) was in development from the final proposal, lodged in February 2013, until February 2018 when it was launched. There are five interesting characteristics of this service:

- Overlay Services allowing individual participants to deliver unique experiences for their customer.
- ISO20022 is the messaging protocol; this would be expected to support enhanced data.
- The architecture is based on a central basic infrastructure component, with participating financial institutions (deposit takers) able to act as integrators to support smaller institutions that do not have exchange settlement accounts with the Reserve Bank.
- Transactions will be settled in real-time by the Reserve Bank through a Fast Settlement Service.
- The option for account holders to assign an alias which could be a mobile number.

My expectation is that this Australian service (developed by SWIFT) will take off like a 'runaway train'. This expectation is based on the Osko overlay service being provided by BPay. BPay is the widely utilized Australian bill payment service. The original RTP specification was built on a TPS (transactions per second) rate of 1000.

NPP architecture and the settlement process

The NPP architecture is built on a basic infrastructure, which comprises:

- Standard message flows,
- Fast Settlement Service (FSS),
- Addressing service.

Individual participants are required to have a payment gateway.

The factor of real interest is the NPP settlement approach. The RBA has introduced a Fast Settlement Service (FSS) supporting NPP settlement on a transaction-by-transaction bases.

With an orthodox bilateral network, each participant settles individually with each of the other parties at the end of each settlement period, normally end of day, and this is referred to as 'Deferred Net Settlement'. We are increasingly seeing shorter settlement periods.

With a hub-and-spoke network, the hub calculates the net deferred settlement position for each participant at the end of each settlement period. The NPP is, in effect, a hub and spoke and there is no requirement for a participant to have a relationship with any other participant.

The Australian NPP takes settlement to another level. There is no need for a settlement period. Settlement is continuous, but as Alistair Mclean points out in his paper 'Australia's New Payments Platform – a guide for the international treasurer' (https://blogs.treasurers.org/australias-new-payments-platform-a-guide-for-the-international-treasurer/), published on 5 March 2018, payments are subject to banks having sufficient funds available in their exchange settlement account at the RBA.

The exchange settlement account is partitioned with a specific balance for FSS transactions. Participating institutions are required to maintain this balance to ensure transactions are not declined.

The RBA's 'Fast Settlement Service Information Paper 3 Requirements Phase April 2014' paper states

> Each Exchange Settlement Account (ESA) holder will continue to have only one ESA; however funds within the ESA will be specifically allocated to RITS [The Reserve Bank Information and Transfer System] and to the FSS.

The intriguing point of this approach, if FSS became universal across all of the interbank, electronic payment networks, is that it should see the use of RTGS (Real-Time Gross Settlement) systems decline to a point where the need must be re-examined, in particular, if the intention or circumstances resulted in the decline of the traditional paper-based payment services. There is no reason why the ATM and EFTPOS systems for domestic transactions cannot be settled in a similar manner utilizing the same or their own FSS.

Phasing out of deferred settlement and batch payment processing will change the requirements of a RTGS.

There is no reason why multiple instances of the FSS cannot be operational. Then the single point of failure drops back to the system that supports the exchange settlement account of each participant. Perhaps this further weakness is addressed by the deployment of distributed ledger technology.

The 'Regulations for the New Payments Platform (NPP)' published by NPP Australia Ltd places the responsibility of the settlement service clearly on the RBA, according to clause 3.2 (a);

> Each NPP Participant, Connected Institution and Overlay Service Provider acknowledges that the RBA is responsible for the availability and perform-ance of the FSS, and that NPPA has no responsibility for, and makes no representation or warranty in relation to, the availability or performance of the FSS for settlement of NPP Payments.

Central banks are responsible for the operational performance of such systems as the RTGS, ESAS and CSD, which if they fail do not generally impact retail (consumer and business) payment services. The RBA with NPP is stepping into the front line of payment service delivery. If the FSS has an outage, I can imagine the Australian banks will not hesitate to point the finger at the RBA.

NPP (RTP) payments are assigned a non-repudiation status (the same status as cash) as they are not able to be reversed once the payee's account has been credited. Purists may claim that inter-bank settlement is therefore a prerequisite for a payment to be finalized.

In a number of countries, their proprietary (national) EFTPOS systems support non-repudiation and net deferred settlement. However, the payee, i.e. merchant, does not receive payment (normally) in real-time. There is therefore the oppor-tunity for whatever reason to reverse a payment before settlement, but this is not normally a supported use case. It is important to note that the scheme card payment service supports the ability for cardholders with a legitimate reason to chargeback a payment. These networks do support repudiation.

Is this FSS approach necessary? The orthodox thinking allows the system risk to be managed. This relates to an event where a financial institution is unable to meet its settlement obligations. Imagine receiving a response on your mobile for a RTP, P2P money transfer: 'Transaction Failed, Bank has Insufficient Funds'.

This situation in reality should never happen. In the case of an individual bank's exchange settlement account, FSS balance, dropping to below a predeter-mined limit, you would expect an alert to be generated to avoid a default situ-ation. A process could be in place to transfer funds from the RITS balance of the exchange settlement account to the FSS balance to ensure continuity of the RTP service. In the world of central banking there are processes in place to address such situations without the public being affected, even if there is a run on a bank.

Further it is conceivable that if there is no upper value limit, a single transaction for an unexpected high value could enter the system, exceeding the payer's bank exchange settlement account balance. In such a situation exception processing needs to be supported.

If I had the opportunity to design a RTP/FSS system, I would only loosely link the two systems so the RTP can continue to operate without disruption until the FSS returns to an operational state. This is not to address a shortage of funds situation but to cover service outages. There is also the potential for the TPS loading to increase sharply to a point where the FSS response times degenerate. RTP users receiving time out responses is not a good look.

For this to happen, the RTP to FSS interface needs to support a 'store and forward' functionality, where the RTP can continue to process transactions without needing a confirmation of settlement. In situations where the RTP's overall TPS reaches a level that the FSS cannot keep pace with or the FSS has an outage, transactions should be queued until FSS is able to catch up. For high TPS rates, the delay may be only seconds, outages obviously much longer. There will be situations where the RTP service requires to be suspended because of the systemic risk concern.

These are all situations the Central Bank should monitor and be able to address before the service to financial institutions and their customers is adversely impacted.

Settlement (non-FSS)

Settlement is a subject not discussed by most commentators, possible because it is neither a trendy subject or not fully understood or there is little requiring to be understood.

A payment instruction, regardless of its type will result in one account being debited and another being credited, but if those accounts are at different institutions then interbank settlement must take place.

RTP services (ignoring NPP) are a domestic implementation, based normally on a hub architecture connected to and supported by a Real-Time Gross Settlement (RTGS) system. Although transactions are not settled individually, net deferred settlement positions should be settled during multiple intra-day settlement windows or be initiated when settlement limits are reached.

RTP open to fraud

Barry Kislingbury, Director of Solution Consulting, Immediate Payments, ACI Worldwide, wrote an article 'Unlocking the true value of immediate payments' published on the IL Salone Dei Pagamenti website (www.aciworldwide.com/insights/expert-view/2017/october/unlocking-the-true-value-of-immediate-payments). This article raises the fraud issue with RTP services, specifically for the 'Request to Pay' transactions. Barry states that fraudsters are utilizing details sourced from social media, physical mail and web scrapes to insert themselves without suspicion.

They falsify communications from a known service supplier, such as a builder, and provide fraudulent account details to direct payments to their account, rather than to the genuine suppliers.

Once the funds are in the fraudster's account, the funds – as Barry suggests – can be moved quickly by following up RTP transactions to various other accounts at other institutions. Is there an opportunity here for blockchain? Biometrics could also have a part to play.

Observations

There is an identified merchant need for frictionless payments. Payments should happen as an integrated and seamless component of the buying experience. The nearest the industry has come to achieving this is probably tap and go at the point of sale for low value transactions not requiring PIN entry.

Payers (customers) are using PTM platform services where they have control.

Faster payment or real-time services are being used by payers, as seen by the UK Faster Payment experience.

There is also no technical reason not to use the RTP, Pay Away model at POS. In fact the two models Pay Away and card-based Request and Response could be supported side-by-side at the POS terminal, providing payers with a choice. It would be needed as a transitional strategy.

This could be handled in two ways:

- The merchant terminals have the capability of passing the merchant's details, possibly via NFC or by the payer scanning a QR code using their smartphone. The payer initiates a payment with the merchant receiving a payment confirmation (on their EFTPOS device) from their acquirer, within an acceptable timeframe, similar to a card present transaction.
- An alternative approach, which could be used by e-commerce sites as well as billers, is for a 'Request to Pay Message' to be generated from their charging/ billing system and sent to the payer's mobile providing the payment details. The payer can then generate a standard RTP payment with the payee receiving a notification.

The two methods are very similar with the second more applicable for replacing card-not-present transactions. The first method does not require the purchaser to provide any details to the merchant and reduces any perceived security risk.

Projection

RTP will become the dominant payment service in the next 15 to 20 years on the back of the mobile handset. RTP will initially build its market presence by replacing cheques and being used for lower value direct credits. Total dominance will only come when a robust domestic card replacement process/solution is delivered.

Cross-border transactions are also a hurdle to overcome as consumers become increasingly more borderless. Fraud from identity theft will be a challenge. SWIFT delivering the Australian NPP solution is of interest in terms of where SWIFT takes the system.

Top of the pyramid – settlement

Any national payment system should be seen as a pyramid, with the central bank setting at the top. Then there are banks with settlement accounts and below those are financial institutions who settle through a bank.

In simple terms, individuals have an account at their banks and their bank has an account at the central bank. For an individual to make payment to an entity with an account at another bank, not only does an individual need available funds in their account but their bank also requires funds in their exchange settlement account.

The central bank is responsible for ensuring a stable financial system. The payment sector refers to systemic risk being managed to ensure no payment system disaster impacts the economy.

The Merriam-Webster definition of systemic risk, which is possibly one of the most simplistic to be found, is: 'the risk that the failure of one financial institution (such as a bank) could cause other interconnected institutions to fail and harm the economy as a whole'.

Typically, if customers of an institution lose trust and rush to withdraw their deposits, an event referred to as 'a run on a bank' occurs. In such cases, the bank subject to the run is unlikely to have the liquidity to pay out its depositors, which creates less trust, and which could spread across the whole financial system.

Central Banks – payment system

Central Banks' primary role in payments is to provide the settlement facility (or be the agent) for interbank payments. The primary system to handle interbank payments is the RTGS. Essentially, a payment is considered for real-time gross settlement if it has a high value and is between two parties (bi-lateral) where there is an element of risk. The transfer of funds occurs between the exchange settlement accounts of the two settlement institutions (normally banks) each representing one of the parties.

Normal practice for lower value payment is for them to be settled on a deferred net basis. The net position between the institutions participating in a typical POS network is calculated on a multilateral basis at the end of a settlement period. Traditionally this has occurred at the end of day but to reduce the risk and to improve the timing on such payments as direct debits or credits, multiple settlement windows per business day have been introduced by many central banks.

For central bank settlement, a financial institution requires to have an exchange settlement account. Typically, it is only the larger institutions, offering a comprehensive range of banking services (full banking licence), that have an exchange settlement account. In some countries these would be considered tier one institutions. Tier two and other lesser institutions would have a relationship with a tier one institution for settlement purposes, referred to as indirect settlement.

The criteria relating to who has a settlement account is country specific. Large corporations' responsible for significant domestic and international payments could have a settlement account. Similarly, PSPs could potentially have a settlement account, especially if they are of a significant size and require close central bank oversight. With PSD2 and the requirement for PSPs to meet certain capital requirements, the next step is a settlement account at the central bank with securities requirements, collateral to manage the systemic risk.

The Bank of England has in fact made changes to support non-bank PSPs opening exchange settlement accounts. This will support PSPs to participate in the UK payment schemes. PSPs in most countries currently use a settlement bank, a competitor – it could be claimed – for inter-bank or scheme settlement.

The Bank of England (July 2017) sees the benefits as:

> In the longer term, the innovation which stems from this expanded access should promote financial stability by:
>
> * creating more diverse payment arrangements with fewer single points of failure,
> * identifying and developing new risk-reducing technologies,
> * expanding the range of transactions that can take place electronically and be settled in central bank money,
> * access to UK Payment Schemes for Non-Bank Payments Service Provider.

Expect other central banks to follow this example.

Systems support

The core system for interbank settlement is the RTGS (Real-Time Gross System). Essentially this system manages the gross (single payment instruction) of high value between two parties.

RTGS will also support the settlement of net positions (multilateral) generated from the clearing cycles of lower value payment services such as RTP, cheques, direct debit and credit services, ATM and EFTPOS networks, etc.

The clearing cycles have traditionally been based on business or calendar day, but with the growth of non-repudiated online transactions, such as generated from RTP services, intra-day settlement is increasingly becoming necessary to manage the settlement risk. Allowing non-bank PSPs to have exchange settlement accounts may place further pressure on the need to shorten clearing cycles.

It is important to note that card transactions cleared through the card scheme networks will be settled by those schemes. The card schemes calculate the net position and debit or credit their customers' bank accounts, for which they have authority.

Bibliography

Bank of England (July 2017) *Access to UK Payment Schemes for Non-Bank Payments Service Provider.* www.bankofengland.co.uk/-/media/boe/files/markets/other-market-operations/access-fornonbankpaymentserviceproviders.pdf

Kislingbury, Barry (16 October 2017) *Unlocking the True Value of Immediate Payments.* www.aciworldwide.com/insights/expert-view/2017/october/unlocking-the-true-value-of-immediate-payments

NPP Australia Limited (28 March 2018) *Regulations for New Payments Platform.* www.nppa.com.au/wp-content/uploads/2017/09/NPP-Regulations_v2.0_Public-version_2.pdf

Reserve Bank of Australia (April 2014). *Fast Settlement Service Information Paper 3 Requirements Phase.*

Transaction Network Services (September 2017) *Global Variance in ATM Usage.* www.businesswire.com/news/home/20170912005872/en/TNS-Report-Uncovers-Significant-Global-Variances-ATM

6

REGULATIONS AND STANDARDS

Fundamentals

For various reasons the payments industry is afflicted with a range of regulations and standards.

Standards are necessary to ensure a suitable level of interoperability can be achieved. The backbone of the retail payment systems has been the ISO8583 messaging standard, which has probably served its time and in the next one to two decades should be replaced by ISO20022. However, ISO8583 has infiltrated card payments to such a level that replacing it entirely is unlike to happen quickly. This messaging standard is not the only critical standard and many may say EMV is more important, as are the other standards relating to security of data and account/card holder authentication. It does not matter; they are all pieces of the same jigsaw puzzle.

Swift MT (Money Transfer) messaging has been the dominant standard covering account-to-account payments, especially with respect to international remittances. MT is being replaced by ISO20022 (MX) messages and this will be completed in the short to medium term.

Between ISO8583 and ISO20022 there is also, shall we say, a contest between the card PAN (primary account number) and the IBAN (international bank account number). There is the argument that one is specifically card related and the other is bank account related. Although I would agree with this view, there seems to be the intent, at least by commentators, for the later to replace the former in time.

If RTP systems begin to dominant the market then we will see ISO20022 becoming the dominant messaging standard quicker.

Compliance to the full range of standards is a fundamental requirement for interoperability, rather than compliance to only the messaging standards.

It should be noted that industry regulations generally only have influence over the open loop payment networks/services. A closed loop service, unless of sufficient size in terms of value, will not generally attract the interest of the regulators (mass transit in most countries being the exception); however, there is still an excellent case for compliance. Many mobile operators have developed and implemented non-compliant systems. Many are now finding their attitude of we will do it our way or simple ignorance is now restricting their business options. Smart Communications (Philippines) is an exception, where a compliant system was developed through integration of mobile with a card product and support for bank interfaces.

Regulator interest in cost

In recent years, in many countries, the interchange fees of the card schemes have attracted the interest of regulators. Australia's actions of the early to mid-2000s attracted the attention of the world.

The setting of domestic or regional interchange fees was a scheme responsibility in consultation with the scheme's membership. In most markets the larger issuers are also the larger acquirers, but the issuing side of the business in most banks has the greatest influence. In many markets, the trend is for banks to use third-party acquiring organizations so they are less concerned about acquiring profitability.

The reasoning behind interchange is historical, like most of these card network practices. The thinking behind interchange was to share the cost between issuing and acquiring. For ATMs, it was considered the acquirers (ATM owners) carried the cost burden, whereas for card acceptance by merchants the view was reversed, with the issuers carrying the cost burden.

Although this argument for credit cards had merit in the past, today it has little creditability, especially at the level being charged. Merchants argued that interchange revenue was at least partially if not fully used for funding loyalty programmes. Reasonably, merchants did not consider this was their responsibility and lobbied the regulators.

The Australian regulators (Reserve Bank and Commerce Commission) took action and regulated Visa and MasterCard interchange fees for domestic transactions. They set out what cost could be recovered from merchants and asked the two card schemes to provide their members' actual costs. American Express and what was Diners Club, now Discovery, were not left out but their business model is different.

The Visa and MasterCard merchant total fee, as report by the RBA in its statistics, has fallen from 1.45 per cent in May 2003 to 0.75 per cent in March 2018. For American Express Merchant Service over the same period, it has dropped from 2.51 per cent to 1.42 per cent.

The contra to this is that the EFTPOS merchant service fee (per transaction) has climbed from 2.65 cents in March 2003 to 9.95 cents in March 2018. The EFTPOS network other fees have dropped over the same period from 9.80 cents to 8.06 cents.

The Australian situation is a little confusing to the outsider (and to most insiders I suspect). Many banks issue a combination credit/debit card and it is the account selection that determines which network is used: the card scheme, or EFTPOS (domestic). Even if you select credit for a debit card it will go down the card scheme network based on brand.

The Australian regulators also allowed surcharging for cards. It is assumed the intent was transparency and this delivered the ability for payers to select a card brand that delivered the lowest interchange fee and therefore cost.

To be as polite as I can, permitting surcharging was unwise and a little naive. In general, the retail price assumes cash is the payment method and therefore the cost is included in the price. If you use a payment card then you are paying as if you were paying with cash plus you are being hit with an additional fee, the surcharge. It is a double hit. The payer is not gaining any fee benefit for not using cash, which many consider the most costly payment method. Merchants are likely to add a margin to their merchant discount fees to arrive at their surcharge rate.

The card scheme rules did not permit surcharging but national regulations have negated these rules.

In an ideal world, merchants should have a table of surcharge fees based on the payment methods supported. This means having a surcharge for cash, ideally set by the regulator. E-commerce sites obviously cannot support cash payments, so why surcharge unless the merchant wishes to annoy its customers by advertising lower prices and then adding fees for various services? Airlines are especially good at additional fee charging. European regulators have decided under PSD2 that surcharging will not be allowed. Sanity prevails.

The Australian regulator's intentions were well founded, but by excluding cash their surcharging had no credibility.

A number of years ago I was contracted by an oil company to look at their merchant service fees and advise on the acquirer with which the company should negotiate a new acquiring contract. Essentially the oil company wished to understand the revenue model for the acquirer/issuing banks.

Analysing their card payments, we could determine each bank's level of on-us to not-on-us transaction split. The bank with the highest level of on-us transactions generates the greatest revenue, as it kept all the interchange on its own cards. The numbers were such that the bank with the highest on-us transaction volume could set a merchant service fee below the interchange rate and still make a positive net profit. This would not work out in all markets. It does, however, need to be understood.

In Australia, direct connect routing was introduced at the time the regulator decided to interfere in the market. I am not sure where it originated and it takes us off on a tangent but it is interesting.

Many of the very largest merchants support their own POS network off their own switch. This provides the merchant with the ability to connect directly to the card schemes for authorization and to an acquiring institution for clearing purposes. It also allows the merchant to connect directly to individual large issuers for authorization and clearing. In Australia, where only four banks dominate the market, the direct connect approach makes sense. It also works in Australia because EFTPOS supports a single message service.

For the smaller issuers, the merchants still needed to use the services of an acquirer. The advantage of merchant direct is that, depending on the market, merchants could send directly 80+ per cent of their transactions to their customer's issuer, delivering the ability to negotiate a lower discount fee.

As the interchange rates are reduced, the benefit of this approach is obviously reduced as the cost/benefit balances changes.

Payment Services Directive 2 (PSD2)

The website of SEPA for Corporation states:

> The revised Payment Services Directive (PSD2 – EU Directive 2015/2366) was proposed by the European Commission in 2013, and the objective was to create a level playing field by:
>
> - Standardising, integrating and improving payment efficiency in the European Union
> - Offering better consumer protection
> - Promoting innovation in the payments space and reducing costs
> - Incorporating and providing clarity on the use of emerging payment methods such as mobile payments and online payments
> - Create an equal playing field for payment service providers – enabling new companies to participate in the payments space
> - Harmonise pricing and improve security of payment processing across the European Union
> - Incorporate new and emerging payment services into the regulation
>
> *(www.sepaforcorporates.com/single-euro-payments-area/
> 5-things-need-know-psd2-payment-services-directive/)*

If you hold the view PSD2 is an EU regulation and will not impact the rest of the world, then you may be correct depending on where you live. However, for the so-called developed payment world, excluding perhaps the USA, the Europeans have significant influence on the global direction. Their influence will also flow down to the developing world, as PSD2 will be seen as best practice.

The EU is the leader in payment regulation and the innovator, in my view. The USA, however, makes a lot of noise but its payment practices are not necessarily aligned with the rest of the world, even when we consider the card schemes that originate from that country. EMV is a case in point.

Some thoughts on PSD2

There is a considerable amount of excitement and hype built up around PSD2. PSD2 came into effect in 2018.

There is an underlying expectation that PSD2 will drive in-country and the EU towards faster payment services (RTP) enabling pay-away payments. It is also expected to encourage innovation resulting in the introduction of newer services. One service relates to the merchant direct model using APIs to directly interface with banks.

PSD2 introduces a new or extended set of players, which could be viewed as new names for existing participants; these being Account Information Service Providers, and Payment Initiation Service Providers alongside the existing Payment Service Providers. Obviously, these players, depending on the scope of their service, will require to be networked unless single providers deliver on multiple service levels, which is most likely.

A few countries have already introduced RTP services with the capability of fitting into the PSP2 regulatory framework but not necessarily supporting the array of third-party service providers. These generally have been set up by the existing entrenched players who will potentially have the ability to deliver competition to the card schemes.

The hype associated with PSD2 is concentrated on allowing third party processors to access customer account details through a set of standard APIs. This is apparently going to open up a rich seam of opportunity for the FinTech sector.

As for the FinTech sector accessing customer account information, PSD2 is supporting customer ownership of the information and customers' right to determine who may have access to it. In an environment where users have a heightened awareness of identity theft, I would perhaps suggest this is not a regulation that will be a game changer.

High net worth customers, subscribers to multiple financial services, delivered by multiple institutions, may find this change to be beneficial along with businesses that bank with multiple institutions. Note that I am not a high net worth customer but my bank already provides me with my transactional data, which I can download in the Excel (CSV) format. It works well as input for my tax returns, although I have to initiate the download. I could, in the CSV format, pass it onto a third party but I would not give a third party unfettered access to the data or any of my other personal details.

I may be overreacting but the fraud issue with card transactions relates to the accessibility of readily available cardholder data. Especially from third parties who have held a mass amount of card data in insecure databases. The question must be asked, is PSD2 opening up the doors to mass account holder data being extracted and stored by third parties.

A mortgagee may insist, as a condition of a loan, that they gain access to the mortgagor's account details, particularly the transaction details. I am aware of one mortgagee who provides a budgeting service and requires spending details to track the mortgagor's performance with respect to their agreed budget. The budget has goals built in and if the mortgagor spending is below budget they are rewarded with loan extensions for spending – for example, a holiday.

You can imagine medical insurance companies insisting their policyholders provide details so they can track lifestyle, especially if the data are enriched with the SKU details on what they are purchasing. A premium increase being forced on policyholders if their spending increases on certain food items (i.e. sugar) is above what is recommended.

With mobile handsets doing everything, identity theft will become a major fraud issue. If your mobile can be cloned through the theft of personal data, in part provided by your bank through a third party and part through malware, then we will all be in trouble.

Cardholder protection

For most customers there is an underlying trust element that their bank will protect their personal data from external parties. Banks need to stand up to the regulators to protect this trusted position. I understand the regulators are trying to open the market up to competition. The problem is the new entrants are probably more commercially savvy than the banks and will monetize what assets (data) they collect.

If a PSP is the card acquirer then it should be accessing its merchant account data to authenticate that a merchant is able to initiate a transaction. This PSP will be likely to have no relationship with the card issuing institutions and should have no access to the cardholder's data, apart from what is contained in the transaction they have acquired (which is unencrypted).

The card issuer and custodian of the cardholder's account and personal data is the only institution who should be able to perform cardholder authentication.

Because of the demand for a higher standard in authentication, PSD2 regulation could introduce more friction into the payment process.

At the time of reading up on PSD2 I purchased an airfare from Nice to London. The experience was interesting and, obviously, the authentication process – shall we say – had been enriched but it had also added friction.

On booking the flight I was required to enter my mobile number (of a recently purchased SIM) and on making the payment I obviously had to enter my card number. There is no real issue here, both requests are obviously necessary.

The payment authentication process then sent a security code by text using the mobile number, which I had given the airline; I needed to enter this code into the payment screen. Then I was asked to enter the last four digits of my card number, which I had just given them. This process was friction, plus it had no possible purpose. Obviously the airline had shared the mobile number with the PSP.

If my card number and mobile number were both on file then I could see a purpose in this authentication. They could have gone back to my card issuer to request my mobile number and then sent the security code to that number, ignoring what I had provided. The last four digits of the card number request was simply a waste of time. I had just given them the full card number.

This authentication process should have been managed by my card issuer using data it already has on file.

If somebody had stolen my card details or the card itself they could have passed through this authentication process using their own mobile number.

Is this the type of process we can expect with PSD2?

While writing this book, the Facebook situation developed. On 26 March 2018, the *Australian* newspaper published an article entitled 'ABA fears for open banking security'. This article stated:

> The Australian Banking Association says the industry is committed to the success of an open banking regime but in the wake of the data breach scandal engulfing Facebook it is concerned about data privacy and security for banking customers.

Anna Bligh, the ABA CEO, was reported as saying,

> Our No 1 area of concern is around customers understanding what they are consenting to and what their data will be used for. Banks take data privacy and security very seriously.

The Facebook situation is a warning to the payment sector. Will the payment regulators take note?

GDPR privacy laws

Perhaps all is not lost. PSD2, delivering access to banking data to third parties, is countered by another regulation. The General Data Protection Regulation (GDPR) has fortunately restricted third parties on how they can use and retain our data. What is the saying, 'one hand gives and the other takes away'? Or am I being cynical?

GDPR took effect on 25 May 2018 to standardize legislation across all the European countries. To quote from the *Official Journal of The European Union*, 4 May 2016, the regulation states:

> The principles of, and rules on the protection of natural persons with regard to the processing of their personal data should, whatever their nationality or residence, respect their fundamental rights and freedoms, in particular their right to the protection of personal data. This Regulation is intended to contribute to the accomplishment of an area of freedom, security and justice and of an economic union, to economic and social progress, to the strengthening and the convergence of the economies within the internal market, and to the well-being of natural persons.

This regulation is extensive and can be accessed through the website http://gdpr-legislation.co.uk/. The following are considered the headline implications to the payments sector:

• Consent is required from the natural person to whom the data relates (owns the data) to access, process and store the data.

- The data captured must be for a specific stated purpose and used only for that purpose.
- The data are required to be corrected if inaccurate and must be kept up to date.
- The data must be deleted once the purpose or need has been satisfied.

An Australian Broadcasting Commission (ABC) website article by Emily Piesse makes the point:

> Given the GDPR is a European law, it would seem to have little relevance for Australia. But any company with customers in the EU will be affected.
>
> *(www.abc.net.au/news/2018-05-08/*
> *gdpr-privacy-laws-could-affect-data-safety/9736258)*

Emily Piesse also quotes Ms Johnstone, director of a Sydney-based consultancy Salinger Privacy:

> Any business that operates online and allows customers to pay with euros, or translates its website into a European language, may fall under the remit of the GDPR.
>
> *(www.abc.net.au/news/2018-05-08/*
> *gdpr-privacy-laws-could-affect-data-safety/9736258)*

Obviously, if this is correct for Australia it is correct for all countries. Ms Johnstone is further quoted by Emily Piesse:

> My clients in Australia are being pressured by their Customers in the US to make sure that they're going to meet the GDPR, because it's simply seen as almost a de facto, new global standard.
>
> *(www.abc.net.au/news/2018-05-08/*
> *gdpr-privacy-laws-could-affect-data-safety/9736258)*

This comment is also of significance as it implies that European Union regulations are impacting the global payment sector, with the EU taking up a leadership role with regulations and standards: GDPR, PSD2, ISO20022, etc.

Impact of new regulations

Europeans, as we all appreciate, have a liking for regulations. As a general statement, a new regulation normally increases barriers to entry and additional compliance demands on participants, simply translating into higher costs and therefore leading to industry consolidation.

Under PSD2, third-party payment providers will need to be registered, satisfy capital requirements and hold professional indemnity insurance. Security will need to be strengthened and customer dispute procedures upgraded with more favourable rights for customers.

GDPR is far broader than the payments sector and the finance industry but has major implications for both. The penalties are significant; some may see them as extreme. There is an element of uncertainty, especially with the GDPR, until we see how the courts apply the legislation.

I have a real problem with the above, although I recognize the need to protect peoples' privacy, especially in this age of data harvesting. These regulations will play to the strengths of the existing players and deter new entrants and therefore will not improve the competitive aspects of the system. In simple terms, regulations may be defeating their purpose. Perhaps I need to be more optimistic?

Payment Card Industry – Data Security Standard (PCI-DSS)

PCI-DSS is another set of processes to plug the holes in the 'request and response' payment model of the card payment method.

The PCI Council was founded in 2006 by American Express, Discovery, JCB International, MasterCard and Visa Inc., as equal participants. Individual card schemes are responsible for their participants' compliance with the standard.

PCI position:

> Maintaining payment security is required for all entities that store, process or transmit cardholder data. Guidance for maintaining payment security is provided in PCI security standards. These set the technical and operational requirements for organizations accepting or processing payment transactions, and for software developers and manufacturers of applications and devices used in those transactions.
>
> *(www.pcisecuritystandards.org/pci_security)*

Many of the objectives of PCI-DSS are business as usual in my experience for the payment industry (as operated by the banks) in the majority of countries in which I have completed assignments, whether you categorize the individual countries as developed or developing economies.

The need for PCI has, in part, been the result of the card industry supporting third-party processes. PSPs, on behave of retailers and billers, have a need for 'card on file' to support recurring payments.

In most cases, banks' primary business is not dominated by cards. Cards are an element of their retail and business banking operation, but they also have corporate and wholesale banking services, which have a high net worth. Cards benefit from the infrastructure built for all these other services, including the security elements. In simple terms, security is in bankers' DNA.

The need for PCI-DSS really originated from both the growth in e-commerce and the growth of 'card on file'. Non-banking institutions, whether retailers or billers, and the emergence of PSPs have resulted in card details being stored insecurely. This is due in part to ignorance of the payment industries' standards and best practices.

My proposition is that increasing the involvement (or operational scope) of PSPs may introduce an increase in the problems associated with data protection. PSPs come in all forms and take on services that banks have lost interest in undertaking, the services banks consider being non-core or they consider others can undertake more efficiently. Obviously, the problem varies by market and not all PSPs in any specific market are ignorant or irresponsible. There are many responsible and professionally managed PSPs.

We have also seen processing organizations emerge on the issuing side of the business again, with banks going down the outsourcing or hosted model, plus, more recently, quasi financial-institutions becoming issuers. One might say that when the barriers to the closed club were breached, so the need for PCI arose.

The point is that the card payments sector has become very fractured and diverse. The criticism I have of PCI is that it was initiated at least 10 years too late and for that the card schemes are responsible. This industry needs a crisis for it to address an issue.

PSPs have introduced innovation, addressed unsatisfied needs while reducing the processing cost. The question is, has this growth in PSPs led to fraudulent activity?

Core requirements of PCI

To gain a detail of understanding of the scope of PCI, it is recommended to read *PCI DSS Quick Reference Guide version 3.2* (PCI Security Council, n.d.). PCI takes what it claims is a common-sense approach based on the principals of best practice.

Core to this, using PCI's words, are:

- Build and maintain secure network and systems.
- Protect cardholder data.
- Maintain a vulnerability management program.
- Implement strong access control measures.
- Regularly monitor and test networks.
- Maintain an information security policy.

Cardholder data elements

A key element of the PCI is the storing of the primary account number (PAN or card number) in an unreadable form. I can understand this requirement if you are also storing cardholder name and expiration date. It is the combination of the three that creates the risk as PANs on their own have little value. They can be generated by the millions if you have a card number generator on your computer. If you are patient then a calculator can be used.

The rationale is possibly that PANs can be easily encrypted.

There is also the requirement to only print the last four digits of the PAN on receipts. A receipt I looked at recently also printed out the bank and card type. This gives any fraudster the capability of aligning the first six digits with the last four, leaving the middle six to be derived. With the check digit being the last digit of the PAN, the number of valid unknown digits is limited.

With EMV, the scope for card-present fraud has been reduced considerably. If card validation codes are not permitted to be captured and therefore are not being stored, plus if 3DSecure is being used appropriately, then card not present fraud is also restricted.

I am not suggesting that card numbers should be not be protected. What I am suggesting is the protection of the authentication data is more critical and it should not be stored under any circumstances. This covers all of Track 2 data, the card validation codes and PINs.

PCI domains

There are four PCI domains; PCI-DSS is the most commonly referred to by the industry because it covers the processing, storage and transmission of data. This does not means the other domains are not equally important.

PCI-PTS covers acceptance devices. This affects the merchant's POS device and, in terms of card present transactions, represents the front door into the networks.

PCI PA-DSS covers the software that processes and stores payment data.

PCI Card Production Logical and Physical Security Requirements relate to card production and personalization processes.

In-market regulatory bodies

The payment industry is required to balance competition and cooperation. In a single word, 'interoperability' requires cooperation on standards, especially for the open loop payment networks.

Regulators are continuously theorizing, conceptualizing and strategizing on how to address common challenges to ensure their national payment system's integrity is maintained. The trust and cost factors are particularly important along with inclusivity.

The industry participants need to ensure changes in regulations can be implemented in a practical manner.

The industry must also coordinate the introduction of change in a manner to minimize any disruption to the overall payment system.

Payment associations or councils have therefore been established in a number of countries. Membership in these bodies is usually voluntary and the associations have no direct authority over their members. They achieve their objectives through consensus and cooperation.

Each country normally establishes these organizations based on their need and the manner in which they conduct business. The Australian example provides a view of the role of these organizations.

The Australian Payments Network, previously the Australia Payment Clearing Association (APAC) defines its purpose and role:

> Australian Payments Network champions the payments system. We enable competition and innovation, promote efficiency, and control and manage risk to deliver improvements for all users of the payments system.
> With a strong focus on collaboration, our role includes:
>
> * inspiring innovation
> * facilitating self-regulation
> * coordinating system-wide standards
> * policy development
>
> Our network includes more than 120 members and participants and we welcome involvement from all organisations with a significant interest in payments.
>
> *(www.auspaynet.com.au/about)*

The Payment System Board of the Reserve Bank of Australia determined they needed to 'foster innovation in the payment system' by addressing the effectiveness of the cooperation between stakeholders and regulators. In consultation with the Australian Payments Network they came up with a new body (additional).

The APC defines its role as:

> The Australian Payments Council promotes industry collaboration. It encourages and facilitates strategic alignment between the payments industry and the Payments System Board on significant payments issues and initiatives. The Australian Payments Council's role is to coordinate industry efforts to:
>
> * Drive the strategic agenda for the Australian payments system
> * Engage with the Payments System Board on setting and achieving strategic objectives
> * Identify strategic issues and emerging trends through constant scanning of the payments environment
> * Generate common industry positions for action and adoption by the industry with the endorsement of the Payments System Board
> * Identify and remove any barriers to innovation through collaboration
>
> The Australian Payments Council undertakes its activities with transparency and integrity.
>
> *(https://australianpaymentscouncil.com.au/)*

In some countries cards are separated into their own associations, as was the case in the UK until 1 July 2017 with the formation of UK Finance.

> UK Finance represents nearly 300 of the leading firms providing finance, banking, markets and payments-related services in or from the UK. UK Finance has been created by combining most of the activities of the Asset Based Finance Association, the British Bankers' Association, the Council of Mortgage Lenders, Financial Fraud Action UK, Payments UK and the UK Cards Association.
>
> *(www.ukfinance.org.uk)*

The key point is that for any country to develop its national payment system, it needs a payment council to drive the direction of the industry to be compliant with regulations and to develop the core networking services to the benefit of all parties and the delivery of interoperability.

Messaging standard ISO20022

The world is moving towards a single standard for all financial messages. That standard is ISO20022, Universal Financial Industry Message Scheme.

To quote SWIFT

> ISO 20022 is a methodology, or recipe, which can be followed when creating financial messaging standards. A global and open standard, ISO 20022 is not controlled by a single interest: it can be used by anyone in the industry and implemented on any network. It has fully established processes for its maintenance, evolution and governance.
>
> First published in 2004, ISO 20022 is widely recognised as the standard of the future. As well as being flexible enough to work with the latest technology, ISO 20022 can also adapt to new technology as it emerges.
>
> *(www.swift.com/standards/about-iso-20022)*

I am strong supporter of standards for a number of reasons:

- When designing a payment solution, using industry standards simplifies the task, reduces the time and provides a level of surety.
- Compliance to the standards supports interoperability between members of the same network. It also opens the network up to new members joining with minimum effort. These types of networks are often referred to as open-loop.
- Even situations where the business case supports a closed-loop network there is a strong case to be compliant to the standards as it future-proofs the investment. Doing so enables the network to integrate/interchange with other parties if the business model changes.

- A compliant system in terms of security provides the feeling the service operator is responsible (trust).

The case for supporting interoperability between networks, even if this is not the immediate business requirement, has been learnt by the mobile money sector the hard way. Ignoring standards, mobile money providers are now (in general) experiencing the consequence of believing they know better, a trap many of us have been caught in.

The ISO20022 standard is heavily embodied with bureaucratic regulations and procedures relating to protecting its integrity. I am of two minds about the necessity of this, considering the likelihood of the card industry doing to this standard what it has done to the ISO8583 standard. Taking a long-term view, will the card schemes, noting they are a power in themselves at some future time, change the standard to satisfy their own requirements?

The rules/processes have been drafted to support quick and urgent amendments to the standard but practice will determine if history is repeated.

The (current) scope of ISO20022

The current status of the standard can be viewed on www.iso20022.org.

Impact of migration

For a new network or service such as RTP, supporting ISO20022 should be the default option if not the only option. The real challenge is to migrate existing networks and services, in particular the card-based delivery channels away from ISO8583. It is not so much the message formats as many, especially EFT, switches are designed to translate messages of varying formats. Many switches work on an internal format for processing all messages, translating from the source format and reformatting them to recipient's format.

At a conceptual level it should be a simple process to manage another messaging standard. An EFT switch should conceptually be able to manage both ISO20022 and ISO8385 formats. The additional data in theory should just involve straight-through processing. However, experience suggests otherwise.

There will be a period where the two messaging standards will have to coexist. The card schemes should have the experience to transition through a migration process. The card system vendors, who are numerous in number, will be impacted possibly more than the schemes. Then there are device vendors who are responsible for capturing, in many insistences, the extended scope of data. If they do not capture the extended data then the exercise becomes a little pointless. For the transitional period EFT switches receiving extended data can simply drop the data in their ISO20022-to-ISO8583 conversion prior to forwarding messages to their non-compliant card management system.

There is the suggestion that an interim step is to support a XML version of ISO8583. I am not sure I understand the rationale for this approach. If you are migrating to ISI20022 then do it.

ISO8583

For the retail payment space, specifically for cards, ISO8583 has been the messaging standard the industry has followed. It was made up of the message categories given in Table 6.1.

The messages are designed with a bit map(s) to indicate what data elements are present. A message could have two-bit maps.

Although ISO8583 is a standard, there are different versions deployed with variations within those versions. The three official versions are identified by their year of release, 1987, 1993 and 2003. Individual networks have created their own versions. As a rule, the core data elements are consistent but variations occur in what could be referred to as the transaction specific data. Between the card schemes in particular there are inconsistencies making it difficult to map their messages on to each other. This is a task that you would not normally need to perform unless you are planning to route messages from one scheme through the network of the other, which on one occasion I had the need to do.

Further, the original message maps supported discretionary data elements. The card schemes again have used these data elements. There is no real scope to send additional data in the ISO8583 messages if your requirement is to comply with a scheme format. While at Visa Asia Pacific, I was involved in the exercise of adding the EMV required data elements. Visa was keen to add a third bit map, which would have not only easily solved the EMV challenge but provided space for additional data. However, this approach was rejected by the other stakeholders and EMV was squeezed into whatever space was available.

It is time to replace ISO8583, but expect a 10-year transition period.

ISO20022 card payment transactions

The following has been sourced from:

> www.iso20022.org/sites/default/files/documents/general/ISO20022_Business Areas.pdf

TABLE 6.1 ISO8583 messages

ID	Description
X1XX	Authorization message
X2XX	Financial messages
X3XX	File action message
X4XX	Reversal and chargeback message
X5XX	Reconciliation message
X6XX	Administrative message
X7XX	Fee collection message
X8XX	Network management message

Those who have defined ISO20022 relate their transactions to a business process, where ISO8583 is more function specific. The term for point of interaction (POI) is a catch-all for all points of interaction between cardholder and the payment service except ATMs. Are ATMs not also points of interaction?

The messages that are supported are:

- Acceptor to acquirer card transactions
- Acquirer to issuer card transactions
- Sale to POI card transactions
- ATM card transactions
- POI management
- ATM management
- Fee collection
- Payment token management
- Network management
- File management
- Settlement reporting
- Fraud reporting and disposition

We must recognize that a considerable amount of effort and patience goes into the development of standards but I question, could not the card-related parts of ISO20022 be perhaps generic? The card messages are supporting the 'Request and Response' payment model described in this book. Request and Response is not exclusively a card payment method and another payment instrument could be deployed that is not a card or not emulating a card. It is just a case of future-proofing the standard.

Conversely, cards could be used in the Pay Away model as well.

The following two websites should be consulted for more details:

www.iso20022.org/full_catalogue.page
www.iso20022.org/cards_standards_evaluation_group.page

EMV

Through mass transit and the Smart City type deployments, smart cards had become locked into the closed loop environments. They had not made any serious impact on the open loop card payment world. They had not made any serious impact on the open loop card payment world, mostly because the user proposition was not strong. There were plenty of ideas and entrepreneurs willing to seek their fortune, resulting in the smart card landscape being littered with commercial failures.

That was until scheme-card-present fraud reached the point where a solution was required. Up until this point, fraud was considered a cost of doing business, a line item in the budget and financial reports.

The card schemes nevertheless struggled to implement EMV globally. The main impediment was the need to upgrade or replace all POS terminals. In many countries merchants either own or lease their devices. This was a significant hurdle for Australia, where 80 per cent of the retail market is owned by a small number of businesses, anecdotally suggested to be six. Such a small base of market ownership represents serious collective power and resistance to a solution for a problem they do not own.

The card schemes forced EMV on what was their members and now their clients through regulation, and the liability shifted from issuers to acquirers.

The most significant deployment that made the industry take notice was the UK's chip and PIN rollout. It needs to be pointed out that this deployment did not move the UK card payment service ahead of the game (as the UK payment sector may claim), in fact it brought the market up to date. Chip and PIN was a deployment of a superior technology platform but not the deployment of a superior business solution.

Up to this point, UK cardholders signed dockets/receipt copies when paying by card. In other, more advanced, markets PINs were being used. It could be termed magnetic stripe and PIN, with PINs being suitably encrypted as part of a PIN block by the POS terminal's tamper-proof PIN pad. PINs were validated at the issuer's switch or host using hardware security modules (HSMs) where the PIN keys were stored securely and the response is only a yes or a no. The difference being that the UK used the capabilities of the chip to validate PINs. PINs are not required to be transported through the network.

The PIN and magnetic stripe cards have also migrated to chip, so they became Chip, PIN and magnetic stripe cards. As a rule, the PIN validation remained at the host and had not migrated to the chip.

One of the issues is ease of managing PINs, allowing cardholders to change their PIN as and when they wish and supporting card reissuance with the same PIN. It also impacts cards continuing to be accepted in a magnetic stripe only environment such as an ATM network (although in many markets ATMs are required to be EMV capable). The ability to validate a PIN on the chip and at the host is feasible assuming the two environments are synchronized.

In situations where a chip card is not enabled to validate the PIN and the network is not capable of transmitting PINs then the fall-back is a signature. There is a strong argument to discontinue this fall-back position in the markets were EMV is fully supported. We can expect magnetic stripes to disappear from cards in the short-term. This process may have already been started by some issuers.

The UK Cards Association in its report, *10 Years of Chip & PIN: 2006 to 2016* states:

> Types of fraud on UK-issued cards, which Chip & PIN was designed to tackle, have fallen since 2004, with counterfeit card fraud down 63 per cent to £47.8 million, lost and stolen card fraud down 48 per cent to £59.7 million and card non-receipt fraud down 86 per cent to £10.1 million in 2014.

It should be made clear that chip and PIN is only relevant to the card-present environment. The card-not-present environment remains a fraudster's paradise.

Basic concepts of an EMV transaction

The following is a brief description of what occurs when an EMV card is inserted into a POS device to complete the payment.

- Card must be inserted and remain in the device for the duration of the transaction.
- Data is exchanged between card and device to initiate the transaction.
- The terminal risk management is performed if there is the option to go online.
- PINs, if supported, can be validated either offline or online.
- The card's chip generates a unique cryptogram which is sent to the host for verification.
- Online request message contains additional EMV specific data.
- Additional processing is required by the Front End Process (FEP) to verify the request cryptogram, generate a response cryptogram, and interrogate additional EMV-specific fields in the request message.
- Online response message contains additional EMV-specific data.
- Issuers are able, in the response, to send scripts for updating the EMV chip.
- Data is exchanged between card and device at the end of the transaction.

Tap and go transactions do not require the card to be inserted into the device but there is a time requirement to support the transfer of data. PIN validation is not a requirement and script processing is not performed.

In a number of implementations, if the value of the transaction exceeds the maximum value for a 'tap and go' payment, a PIN is requested by the device and is sent to the issuer for authentication.

Bibliography

Australian Payments Council (n.d.) *About Us*. http://australianpaymentscouncil.com.au

Australian Payment Network (n.d.) *About*. www.auspaynet.com.au/about

ISE20022 Universal financial industry message scheme (n.d.) *ISO 20022 Business Areas*. www.iso20022.org/sites/default/files/documents/general/ISO20022_BusinessAreas.pdf

O'Dowd, Cliona (2018) ABA fears for open banking security. *The Australian*, 26 March.

PCI Security Council (n.d.) *PCI DSS Quick Reference Guide, Understanding the Payment Card Industry, Data Security Standard version 3.2*. www.pcisecuritystandards.org/documents/PCIDSS_QRGv3_2.pdf

PCI Security Council (n.d.) *PCI Security*. www.pcisecuritystandards.org/pci_security/

Piesse, Emily (8 May 2018) *New GDPR Privacy Laws Triggering Data Emails from Twitter, eBay and Others Include Huge Fine*. www.abc.net.au/news/2018-05-08/gdpr-privacy-laws-could-affect-data-safety/9736258

SEPA for Corporates (13 October 2015) *5 Things You Need to Know About PSD-2 – Payment Service Directive*. www.sepaforcorporates.com/single-euro-payments-area/5-things-need-know-psd2-payment-services-directive/

SWIFT (n.d.) *About ISO 20022. The Standard of the Future.* www.swift.com/standards/about-iso-20022

The Official Journal of the European Union (4 May 2016) *Regulation (EU) 2016/679 of the European Parliament and of the Council of 27 April 2016.* https//gdpr-legislation.co.uk

UK Cards Association (n.d.) *10 Years of Chip & PIN: 2006 to 2016.* www.theukcardsassociation.org.uk/wm_documents/10%20Years%20of%20Chip%20%20PIN%20report%20%282%29.pdf

UK Finance (n.d.) *About Us –Who Are We.* www.ukfinance.org.uk/

7

THE SLOWLY SHIFTING SANDS OF PAYMENTS

The rationale

As payment industry participants developing solutions for the next decade or two, we need to understand where our users, the people, are taking us. There is little profit in building solutions requiring a significant shift in user behaviour.

Two factors that must be understood:

- The level of new transactions entering the electronic payment ecosystem.
- Transaction migration within the electronic ecosystem.

The UK market has been chosen for an insight into user direction. This is for two simple reasons:

- The various payment associations publish comprehensive data.
- The UK is currently the most developed market with its faster payment service (RTP) now having been in operation for near on 10 years.

So what can we learn?

To be able to compare one year with another it is critical to neutralize population growth. The active levels should be based on a per inhabitant basis.

It is also important to understand the level of new transactions that are entering the electronic payment system. Typically these would be cash transactions being substituted with an electronic payment method plus new transactions being generated from economic growth.

I have concentrated on the payment method rather than the payment channel. It is recognized there is not always an absolute demarcation between the two.

When is mobile a payment channel or a payment method or a payment instrument's form factor? No model is perfect.

The eco-system has been limited to the following payment methods:

- BACS
- CHAPS
- Cheques
- Faster payments – immediate
- Faster payments – non-immediate
- Debit card – retail purchases
- Credit card – retail purchases

The original thinking was to include ATMs but, after consideration, they were ruled out as they support cash payments and at a channel level strictly a user interface.

BACS, using its own words as published on its website, describes itself as;

> BACS is the company which runs Direct Debit in the UK. We also run the BACS Direct Credit Scheme, which is used to pay salaries and settle invoices from suppliers; this is commonly referred to just as BACS.

This is not the most exciting processing and a long way from the leading edge represented by the world of RTP and mobile-initiated payments. The volumes though are very high, at 6.2 billion transactions in 2016.

CHAPS is the real-time settlement of high value payments and the volume is, in comparison with BACS, quite modest.

Faster payments – non immediate, are those that go through the faster payments service and which are delayed, including standard orders.

New transactions

The growth in the infrastructure based on transactions per inhabitant between 2009 and 2016 was 57 per cent – 234 transactions per inhabitant to 368 per inhabitant in 2016. The 2012 downturn in the UK economy is reflected by little growth for that year. The slowing in economic activity will cause lower growth in 'per inhabitant payment transactions' as people initiate fewer payments or they are less inclined to change their payment method. They also may revert to using cash more frequently.

Figure 7.1 indicates an average 6 per cent movement (growth) per inhabitant as the norm although, logic would suggest a lowering of this figure over the longer term.

This growth rate is below those reported in the *2016 World Payments Report*, jointly compiled by Capgemini and BNP Paribas (2016). This estimated the 2015 non-cash volumes will grow globally by 10.1 per cent. Growth for 2014 was 8.9 per cent.

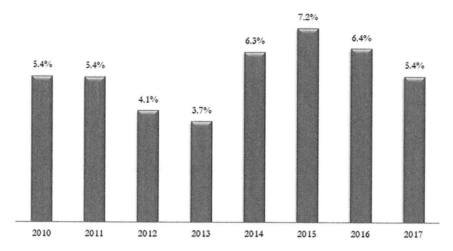

FIGURE 7.1   Growth of electric payments over previous year – UK

Source: Data from Finance UK Statistics.

For the UK, this report states the growth for the number of non-cash trans-actions per inhabitant, for the period 2010–2013 at a CAGR of 5.1 per cent, while for 2013–2014 growth was 7.3 per cent. These rates are above but not wildly different from those I have calculated (Figure 7.1). The corresponding rates for Australia are 7.3 per cent and 6.4 per cent. China is at the other end of the spectrum at 30.7 per cent and 46.2 per cent respectively.

The impact of contactless, tap and go, needs to be considered in countries where cards are not used for low-value transactions. Low-value transactions are, in many markets, the domain of cash but this is under threat as adoption rates for contactless increase. One could argue that once tap and go is fully accepted growth rates will drop.

Transaction transition

With the Faster Payment service having been introduced into the UK in 2008 it is interesting to see how this has impacted the transaction mix by payment method (Figure 7.2).

The two dominant payment methods are BACS and debit cards (Figure 7.3).

In the period 2009 to 2017 there is significant movement in the UK with respect to payment method usage. Debit cards have more than half of the market. Credit cards have declined 1.6 per cent. BACS and Cheques have dropped significantly.

Figure 7.4 demonstrates where the growth has been. It must be recognized for both categories of Faster Payments that growth is impressive but is off a very small base. BACS has stayed still and cheques are going out of fashion. Debit cards sustain strong growth.

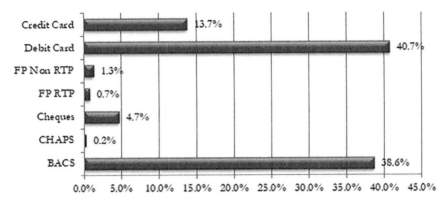

FIGURE 7.2   Payment method usage by inhabitant 2009 – UK

Source: Data from Finance UK Statistics.

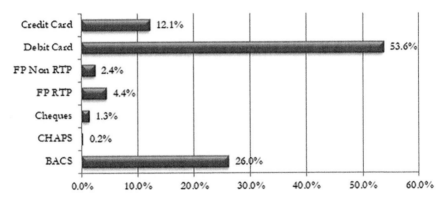

FIGURE 7.3   Payment method usage by inhabitant 2017 – UK

Source: Data from Finance UK Statistics.

Projection 2026 – UK

The trend has been projected from the last five years of movement to neutralize Faster Payment – RTP initial growth (Figure 7.5). Based on the trend, cheques will, in effect, disappear even if the banks do not pull cheques earlier. The BACS market share will also decline significantly, down to 15 per cent.

Faster Payments – RTP will see a significant but more normal growth, up to 13 per cent. This growth will come from cheques and BACS transactions. Legacy payments are naturally the big losers. Debit and credit cards will hold their ground.

What about mobile payments? Mobile NFC is still a card. The form factor and user interface has changed, but the transaction still goes down the card rails. Faster payments may be initiated from a mobile handset, a PC or a tablet but it is still a faster payment.

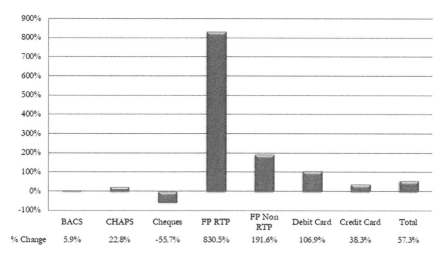

FIGURE 7.4   Payment method movement – UK 2009–2016

Source: Data from Finance UK Statistics.

What about cryptocurrencies? Bitcoin currently does not qualify as a mass-market payment service. It needs to be watched and has the potential to influence CHAPS and Faster Payments – RTP and their equivalents in other countries. High-value cross-border or international payments is possibly a segment where cryptocurrencies could replace US$ as the international trading currency.

A cryptocurrency needs to be endorsed by various regulators for it to become legitimate. Legitimacy will lead to acceptance (and trust), a prerequisite to being used broadly. If this happens, then we can expect to see cryptocurrency payments being supported from a faster payment service.

Debit cards and Faster Payments (immediate) will account for 75 per cent of the market. For the FinTech evangelists, this is where your potential fortune is likely to be found.

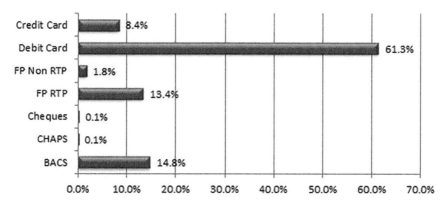

FIGURE 7.5   Payment method usage, 2026 projection

As credit and debit cards in terms of acceptance are increasingly becoming supported from the same channels then the RTP/debit card share of 75 per cent, with the inclusion of credit cards increases to 83 per cent.

Will the card channels become dominant? The answer is probably not.

Business payments will move from the traditional batch payment methods to Faster Payments as authorities increase the maximum value limits. This shift is represented in this projection. The potential for card transactions to be migrated to Faster Payments is dependent on the payment industry (FinTech sector) to build a retail payment channel. A channel that erodes card present and card not present transactions, by being able to integrate reasonably seamlessly into existing retail services, is the challenge. It is hard to accept that a differential in market share of 48 per cent will be reached between these two payment methods.

What is clear is batch and cheque payment processing are in their sunset years. Cheques will be the first to go and batch will be around for some time. The corporate systems that produce batch payment files will need to be replaced, enhanced or individual transactions be processed individually by the RTP service, potentially in non-peak periods.

However, the FP non RTP payments, which sounds like a contradiction, will have a significant contribution in 2026. The development of this category beyond standing orders will impact batch processing.

Impact of APIs

The impact of the provisioning of APIs is currently unclear. Potentially this will introduce another category of payment, which we may refer to as being direct or off channel.

Bibliography

BACS (n.d.) *BACS*. www.bacs.co.uk
Capgemini and BNP Paribas (2016) *2016 World Payments Report*. www.capgemini.com/resources/world-payments-report-2016

APPENDIX

Terms and concepts

In the payments industry there are many terms and concepts, often with alternative meanings. It is important to understand the author's understanding or definition to minimize any confusion.

TABLE A.1 Terms and concepts

Term	Explanation
Acquiring	Acquiring refers to the process of sourcing card transactions from merchants and presenting the not-on-us transactions to the scheme operator for settlement.
	Acquirers manage their merchants, paying them for the value of their transactions less the commission.
	Acquirers are required to manage their merchant base, dealing with any disputes and providing support. Fraud prevention and compliance to standards are also two areas requiring attention.
Automatic Clearing House (ACH)	ACHs were established to manage the exchange of transaction files between banks for clearing and settlement purposes.
	Part of the process involves the electronic capture of cheques to enable the clearing process. An electronic representation of the payment is created to enable transaction processing and interchange. The paper instruments were originally sorted for return to the account-owning branch.
	This has been updated with the introduction of truncation and the capture of payment instrument images to reduce the need to handle the paper.
	A clearing house handles electronic transactions such as automatic payments, standing orders, direct debits and credits, etc. In some countries payment card (financial) transactions are processed in a batch format by clearing houses.
	End-of-day financial settlement positions are generated for the participating institutions. Clearing houses may generate interim settlement positions. Inter-day settlement is becoming more common where a RTGS system can be utilized.
	Clearing houses also need to handle exception transactions resulting from dishonours, closed accounts etc.

continued

TABLE A.1 Continued

Term	Explanation
BIN	Bank Identification Number, traditionally six digits, but variable BIN lengths are supported. The BIN makes up the first digits of the PAN or card number and is unique to the card issuing institution.
	An issuer can have multiple BIN numbers for different card products and will if issuing multiple card brands. Originally the first and second digits of the BIN reflected the card scheme. The pressure on BIN availability along with the branding of proprietary cards this structure has gradually collapsed.
	The BIN underpins the routing of a payment instruction from the point of acceptance to the issuer.
	The term BIN is being substituted by IIN, Issuer Identification Number.
Card products	The expansion of card types has been a marketer's dream. A type classifies cards with similar product attributes and features. A key attribute that determines type and therefore the marketing label placed on the plastic (form factor) is the supporting account classification.
	The common card types are:
	• Credit card – linked to a revolving credit facility (account).
	• Charge card – linked to an account that is expected to be paid off in full on due date.
	• Debit card – normally linked to a bank account(s) that may be known as a current account, DDA, savings etc.
	• Prepaid card – linked to an account established for a specific purpose, not necessarily managed by a bank and through regulation may have limitations imposed in terms of usage and a maximum balance.
	• Gift card – essentially a replacement for the old retailer's paper based gift voucher. Due to the technology and available payment options these cards are as would be expected, not as restrictive as the old vouchers.
	• Travel card – The card industries answer to Traveller's Cheques. As with gift cards the technology and available payment options means these cards offer more than the traditional cheque.
	Cards issued for a closed loop network are referred to as proprietary. The Visa, MasterCard, CUP, JCB, American Express, Discovery (Diners Club), etc., are referred to as scheme or branded.
	Banks in selective markets have pursued a one-card strategy for their core card products. This is where multiple accounts are linked to the one card although this is only fully applicable in domestic markets. The account selected determines the card type.

Card tracks (magnetic stripe)	Payment cards that comply with the standards will support three tracks on their magnetic stripe. Tracks 1 and 2 are covered by ISO7813.
	On both tracks are the Primary Account Number, Expiry Date and Service Code.
	In addition:
	Track 1 (79 alphanumeric characters) holds the Cardholder Name + discretionary data.
	Track 2 (40 numeric characters) is consider the critical track as it again holds card primary account number, expiry date, service code, plus discretion data that is normally taken up by the PIN offset and/or PIN verification value (PVV), CVC1/CVV1.
	The discretionary data areas have been largely claimed by the cards schemes. For private label cards these remain discretionary.
	Track 3 is covered by ISO4909. The financial industry rarely uses this track. As the only read/write track, banks may hold account usage data on this track to support offline transactions. This is no longer a practice that is commonly deployed.
	With the universal adoption of EMV cards, magnetic stripes have a limited future.
Chargeback	A method of challenging a card transaction by returning the transaction back to the acquiring institution for proof of authenticity.
	Cardholders initiate this process by lodging a request with their card issuer. Card issuers will initiate this process when they detect fraudulent transactions, often if they have the capability, automatically.
Correspondent bank	A bilateral relationship is between two banks, in separate jurisdictions, enabling cross territorial payments.
Delivery channels	A delivery channel covers the logistics of transferring payment instructions from the point of initiation or acceptance to the institution that has acquired the transaction. The payment form factor and instrument often determines the channel. Channels have been developed to enable a specific payment instrument and payment instructions to be accepted and processed.
	Common delivery channels are:
	• ATMs (Automatic Teller Machines) networks
	• POS (Point of Sale) networks
	• Telephone banking services
	• Internet direct payments
	• Mobile money

continued

TABLE A.1 Continued

Term	Explanation
EMV (Europay, MasterCard, Visa)	A chip standard that supports open loop payment networks but not exclusively. EMV is managed by EMVco a consortium between, MasterCard, Visa, Discovery, JCB and American Express.
	The schemes provide standard payment applications that are EMV certified. Individual issuers can load their own proprietary applications and data. Such an example is biometric authentication of cardholders.
Feature phone	A term used to categorize non-smartphones. Mobile handsets that pre-date smartphones. Although feature handsets are declining as a percentage of the total market the number in emerging economies is still of significance.
FinTech	Financial Technology, or FinTech, is a new sector (movement) driving a more open banking industry, using the latest technology. A focus for innovators and investors who are willing to carry a higher risk because of the perceived high returns. Payments are a specific area of the industry being targeted. FinTech and disruption are used often in the same conversation.
	The FinTech sector often is considered to be a collective of small innovative businesses but it does include many large IT companies.
Form factor	A payment instrument, especially with a chip hosting capability can be carried on multiple form factors. The common and traditional form factor is a plastic card but the mobile handset, a key fob, wristwatch, etc., are all options.
	The card form factor can be virtual, no plastic at all just an electronic record.
	A mobile handset supporting NFC, utilizing the secure element on the SIM. A chip similar to that held on a card but NFC enables the handset to be the form factor.
	Cheque is a payment instrument, but the paper it is printed or written on is, in effect, the form factor.
Indian Correspondent Banks (ICB)	ICBs deliver 'no frills' accounts through an agency network by being aligned to one or more of the state banks or a participating private bank. Created to grow financial inclusion.

Mobile	A generic term referring to mobile telecommunications, whether the network or the device. Mobile covers: • The network being used as the telecommunications channel only where a payment device is connecting via a mobile Wi-Fi device. • The handset is a feature phone where an app on the SIM is supporting a payments service. The handset if a Smartphone: • Supporting a payment service either in a dedicated app or as a component of a mobile banking service. • Acting as a card form factor as in NFC, often referred to as a wallet. • Support attachments such as a card reader and PIN pad through a dedicated app.
Non-repudiation/ irrevocable transactions	Non-repudiation or irrevocable transactions are typically those that are finalized in real-time (payer/payees accounts being updated). ATM cash out and money transfer transactions are irrevocable. Proprietary EFTPOS systems are irrevocable although merchants are rarely credited in real-time. RTP transactions are also irrevocable. The payee receiving cleared funds in real-time. The card schemes' transactions are conditionally revocable. Card schemes offer a chargeback service but each transaction has to qualify. In the cases of fraudulent transactions (once proven) the chargeback process ensures the cardholder does not wear the loss. Regardless of a service supporting revocability or not, payers/cardholders can always directly present their case to their financial institution. In countries where there is a third party dispute process such as provided by banking ombudsman, payers/cardholders can seek assistance to resolve a dispute. The game changes if a financial institution cannot cover its settlement position with the other financial institutions.

continued

TABLE A.1 Continued

Term	Explanation
Not-on-us/on-us	For card transactions there are two parties, the merchant acquirer and the card issuer. In many markets the larger financial institutions will fill both roles. An acquirer will receive transactions from their merchant base, initiated by cardholders from a range of institutions, including from their own cardholders. Transactions initiated from their own cardholders are referred to as 'on-us'. Those transaction initiated by cardholders of other financial institutions, (card issuers) are referred to as 'not-on-us'.
Payment instruction	The payment instruction is the content of the message containing a request to make payment. It contains the necessary details relating to payer and payee identifications for authentication/validation, the value to be transferred, plus other relevant details required to accept and process the instruction.
Payment instrument	The payment instrument enables a transaction to be initiated. The instrument enables the initiator to be identified and potentially authenticated. The payment instrument is an access device. Common payment instruments are: • Cash (as it represents value) • Cheque • Payment card • Vouchers • Direct debits/credits • Standing orders and automatic payments There is obviously a cross-over between form factors and payment instruments. This attempt to separate them is useful when developing entity models when designing a network.

Payment networks	These typically handle not-on-us payment transactions that have been accepted by an acquirer.
	Typically, we are speaking about the Visa and MasterCard services when it comes to open loop systems. A number of domestic markets have payment networks open to multiple issuers and acquirers.
	Real-time payment services are built on a payment network.
	The terms *processor* and *network* do cross over. The point of difference is a network will perform settlement.
	The settlement process for card scheme's dual messaging networks involves the transfer of batch transactions at the end of the settlement period. However under the single message protocol, authorization and financial transaction management occurs simultaneously. At the end of the settlement period a reconciliation message containing net settlement totals is exchanged. This has become the default for ATM networks.
	Auxiliary services are also offered relating to payment guarantee and protection services, dispute resolution, etc.
	Members of a network normally are required to provide securities of a type that can be liquidated easily and quickly to cover a negative settlement positions in the case of non-payment.
Payment processors	There is a variety of payment processors, most market specific. The North American model of large acquirers and Independent Sales Organizations are excellent examples of the processing services model. Other markets have similar types of organizations. PSD2 is promoting a broader range of PSPs.
	EFT switches supporting ATM and POS networks owned by a consortium of banks are a common form of processor in many countries. This model allows banks to share the investment and operational costs through sharing devices and aggregating volume.
	The internet and now mobile have given birth to a number of organizations who operate payment gateways.
	The clearing houses are processors with a specific function.
Points of Acceptance	Point of Acceptance is where a payment transaction is initiated. POS devices and ATMs are the most common points of acceptance. Mobile handsets, internet sites and telephones (to use a dated term, MOTO services) are also points of acceptance.

continued

TABLE A.1 Continued

Term	Explanation
RTGS	Real-Time Gross Settlement, central bank system used to clear interbank higher value transactions and settlement positions.
Settlement, deferred versus faster settlement services or real-time	When the two parties in a money transfer transaction bank with different financial institutions, funds must be transferred between the two corresponding parties (financial institutions). For domestic transactions this transfer of funds or settlement process is undertaken through the central bank with the debiting and crediting of the financial institutions exchange settlement accounts.
	Deferred or net deferred settlement is post the transactions completion. For networks such as ATMs where the transaction value is low but the volume is high the settlement positions are netted across the various participating institutions for each settlement period.
	In a higher value transaction where the risk is high or there is urgency, settlement between the financial institutions occurs in real-time using the central banks' real-time gross settlement (RTGS) service.
	For RTP payment services the general approach is still to use net deferred settlement but this could be changing with the introduction of faster settlement services (FSS) where even lower value transactions are individually settled.
	As more transactions are processed electronically and where the transactions are guaranteed (non-repudiation), central banks have introduced multiple settlement windows per day (if a FSS is not supported). Traditionally, settlement only took place at the end of day.

INDEX

Page numbers in **bold** denote tables.